T0384311

# the joy of an
# uncluttered life

# the joy of an uncluttered life

## JOYCE MEYER

New York • Nashville

FaithWords
Hachette Book Group
1290 Avenue of the Americas, New York, NY 10104
faithwords.com
twitter.com/faithwords

First Edition: June 2024

FaithWords is a division of Hachette Book Group, Inc. The FaithWords name and logo are registered trademarks of Hachette Book Group, Inc.

The publisher is not responsible for websites (or their content) that are not owned by the publisher.

The Hachette Speakers Bureau provides a wide range of authors for speaking events. To find out more, go to hachettespeakersbureau.com or email HachetteSpeakers@hbgusa.com.

FaithWords books may be purchased in bulk for business, educational, or promotional use. For information, please contact your local bookseller or the Hachette Book Group Special Markets Department at special.markets@hbgusa.com.

Adapted from *100 Ways to Simplify Your Life*

Library of Congress Cataloging-in-Publication Data has been applied for.

ISBNs: 978-1-5460-4695-0 (paper over board), 978-1-5460-4696-7 (ebook)

Printed in the United States of America

LSC-C

Printing 3, 2024

# CONTENTS

# INTRODUCTION

Many people today live stressed, complicated lives that leave them feeling frustrated, burdened, weary, or burned out. But I have good news: Your life does not have to be this way. You can choose simplicity, fruitfulness, peace, joy, and fulfillment. Life may pull you toward stress and complexity, but you can decide to resist this, commit to an uncluttered life, and take steps that lead to an easier, less frustrating way of living.

I remember complaining to God one time about how crazy my schedule was—and then realizing that I was the one who made my schedule, and I was the only one who could change it. We can all spend our lives wishing things were different, but wishing doesn't accomplish anything. Smart decision-making and decisive actions bring about change. If you picked up this book because you long for a simpler life, I hope you will not only read it, but also act on its advice.

Life can get cluttered in many ways. We can have physical clutter around us, and we can feel cluttered and overwhelmed in our minds and emotions. We can even feel cluttered when we have information overload or when people are talking too much and we just need some time alone. I have come to believe that life cannot be simple and uncluttered unless I approach everything simply. My attitude is what determines how easy or complex any situation will be. If I choose to view things in simple terms, I can deal with them in simple ways. Then they don't become intense or complicated.

There are certainly more than a hundred ways to discover the joy of an uncluttered life, but I hope that reading through the ones I write about in this book will help you develop a mindset of simplicity so you can approach every situation you encounter with a simple perspective. I believe this will dramatically increase the peace and joy you experience in your everyday life. To make this book even easier for you, I've emphasized the one key point of each chapter so you can see it easily and apply it quickly to your life.

Jesus came that we might "have and *enjoy* life, and have it in abundance (to the full, till it overflows)" (John 10:10, italics mine), and I have found that many times, simplicity is an overlooked key to enjoying life. I pray that this book will help you as you live the life Jesus came to give you.

**DAY 1**

# FOCUS ON ONE THING AT A TIME

*Whatever your hand finds to do, do it with all your might.*

**ECCLESIASTES 9:10** NIV

When we do things without focusing on them, we decrease our strength to do the work before us and do it well. When we put our hands to one thing and our minds to another, we make our tasks more difficult than they would otherwise be. But when we direct all our faculties to the one thing we are doing at a particular time, we find it much easier to do. The ability to concentrate and stay focused comes from being disciplined, and we can train ourselves to be this way.

Philippians 4:6 teaches us not to be anxious about anything. Anxious people often spend today trying to figure out tomorrow. Not only do they lose the blessings available in the present moment when they do this; they also give themselves too much to think about. This makes life unnecessarily complicated.

*Practice living one day at a time.* Devote yourself—your thoughts, your conversation, your energies, every part of you—to the day and the tasks at hand. Develop the ability to give yourself completely to what you are doing. This will enable you to enjoy the current activity, instead of dealing with anxiety or confusing thoughts that leave you exhausted.

Do you fear you will not accomplish as much if you try to live this way? It's true you may not do as much, but you will also enjoy what you do a whole lot more.

1

# DISCOVER THE JOY OF CONTENTMENT

*Keep your lives free from the love of money and be content with what you have, because God has said, "Never will I leave you; never will I forsake you."*

**HEBREWS 13:5** NIV

In our affluent Western culture, people seem to crave more and more, yet they don't enjoy what they already possess. People who have discovered the blessings of simplicity are satisfied people; they don't yearn for more of anything, but they do thoroughly enjoy what God has given them. They trust God to meet all their needs (Philippians 4:19), and they believe that more will come to them in due time, according to God's plan for their lives.

The world wants us to believe that having more will make us happy, but this is not true. In fact, the more we have, the more we must do to take care of it. We may think more makes life easier, but in reality, it often complicates our everyday lives. First Timothy 6:6 says that "godliness with contentment is great gain" (NIV), and Philippians 4:11 teaches us that the apostle Paul learned to be content regardless of his circumstances. We should all aspire to this kind of satisfaction.

Let's develop the habit of asking God for what we want and believing He will give it to us if, and when, it is right. This simple approach to living sets us free to *enjoy* life.

*Make the decision to begin thoroughly enjoying what you have.* Thank God for it and be content.

# DAY 3    MAKE GOD YOUR TOP PRIORITY

*"For I know the plans I have for you," declares the Lord, "plans to prosper you and not to harm you, plans to give you hope and a future."*

JEREMIAH 29:11 NIV

According to Psalm 35:27, God takes pleasure in the prosperity of His people, and He actually has plans to prosper us. True prosperity encompasses much more than money and possessions; it means that all our needs are met and that things are going well for us in every area of our lives. I believe God wants our needs to be met and that He desires for us to have the resources we need, many of the things we want, and an abundance to use to bless other people.

We should learn to handle abundance properly by keeping God as our top priority and being diligent in using the blessings we receive to bless others.

God has created us and "gives us richly all things to enjoy" (1 Timothy 6:17 NKJV). We can enjoy abundance without allowing it to pull us away from God. We can be prosperous and still keep Him first in our lives. In fact, I believe God is delighted when He finds someone He can bless generously who will make Him their top priority while also being diligent in blessing other people.

Intentionally being a blessing to others is one of the simple things I enjoy doing. It is a way I can give joy to others, and increase my own joy at the same time. *Don't hesitate to ask God to bless you and make you prosperous. Just keep Him in first place when He does.*

3

# LIVE A LIFE THAT GLORIFIES GOD

*So whether you eat or drink or whatever you do, do it all for the glory of God.*

1 CORINTHIANS 10:31 NIV

We often give God glory through our words or spiritual acts, but it's equally important to glorify Him through the way we live our lives. All of life can be holy if we live for God. Colossians 3:23 says, "Whatever you do, work at it with all your heart, as working for the Lord, not for human masters" (NIV).

God assigns to us the ordinary tasks of life as well as spiritual activities such as prayer, Bible study, good works, and fellowship with other believers. As we study His Word, we can see that we are to work and be good employees, pay our bills, deal honestly, take care of our bodies, keep our homes in order, enjoy the people God puts in our lives, enjoy our food, rest, and laugh. When we begin to see each activity as something we do unto God and for His glory, we simplify our lives. We aren't caught up in trying to *do*; we are simply involved in being who God made us to *be*.

*Begin to simplify your life by cultivating an intimate relationship with God.* Follow His teachings and Christ's example, and love Him for who He is, not just for what He can do for you. This will help keep life uncomplicated and uncluttered.

# DON'T FRET ABOUT THE FUTURE

*Therefore do not worry about tomorrow, for tomorrow will worry about itself. Each day has enough trouble of its own.*

**MATTHEW 6:34** NIV

When we think about the future with its many uncertainties and the seemingly threatening possibilities it holds, we can feel anxious and overwhelmed. This is why God gives us grace for only one day at a time.

Every day we live contains all we can handle. It has its unique challenges, responsibilities, and blessings. God gives us grace to deal with what's in front of us on any given day, not what may come weeks, months, or years later. We may be tempted to fret about the future, but God simply asks us to trust Him day by day.

Trying to live tomorrow today makes life complicated. In Luke 11:3, Jesus teaches us to pray for our "daily bread." Even though He spoke specifically of bread, I believe this refers to whatever it takes to meet our daily needs.

God is always faithful to give us what we need when we need it. He is always on time but rarely early. He will give you what you need for the future. It's impossible to effectively deal with tomorrow's problems today, but when tomorrow comes, you will have the wisdom and resources you need to handle what it brings. *Don't complicate your life by fretting about the future; simplify it by focusing on the present.*

5

## DAY 6

# LEAVE THE PAST BEHIND

*Let your eyes look straight ahead; fix your gaze directly before you.*
**PROVERBS 4:25** NIV

If we want to enjoy a bright and fulfilling future, we must leave the past behind us. We cannot see God's good plan for today or tomorrow if our focus is fixed on yesterday. We can learn from yesterday's mistakes, but we cannot go back and do things over.

When Abram and Lot needed to go their separate ways, Lot chose the best land for himself, leaving Abram with the less desirable land and with much less property than he previously had (Genesis 13:1–12).

Abram could have felt sorry for himself or resented Lot, but instead, he trusted God, who said, "Lift up now your eyes and look from the place where you are, northward and southward and eastward and westward; for all the land which you see I will give to you and to your posterity forever" (Genesis 13:14–15).

Basically, God was telling Abram to look *up* and look *around*. This is good advice for us. We need to look up and around instead of down and behind. *Stop dwelling on what's behind you, and start looking forward to what's ahead.* God has a wonderful plan for your life, and you can trust Him to have good things in store for you. Don't spend your life mourning what you have lost. Instead, take an inventory of what you have left, be thankful for it, and move forward, one step of faith at a time.

# IT'S OKAY TO SAY NO

*Above all, my brothers and sisters, do not swear—not by heaven or by earth or by anything else. All you need to say is a simple "Yes" or "No." Otherwise you will be condemned.*

**JAMES 5:12** NIV

People tend to be happy with us when we say yes to them and unhappy when we say no. We don't enjoy feeling that we have disappointed anyone or being afraid they will reject us if we don't do what they want us to do. For this reason, we are often tempted to agree to do things we really don't want to do or feel God is leading us to do. Trying to please people creates conflict inside of us and clutters our lives. We can greatly simplify our lives by learning to say no when we believe we should.

Commit to please God above all else. Put His will before your own and before what other people want you to do. If you truly feel in your heart that God would have you say yes to something, then say yes and stick to it. *But if you feel He is leading you to say no, then say no kindly and stick to that as well.*

God always supplies everything we need to do what He calls us to do. But He won't give us the strength to do what He doesn't want us to do. If our mouths say yes to something while our hearts are saying no, we cannot expect God to give us peace or joy. But when we follow God's leading, He gives us the grace and strength we need, as well as peace and joy.

7

# YOU BE YOU

*But let every person carefully scrutinize and examine and test his own conduct and his own work. He can then have the personal satisfaction and joy of doing something commendable [in itself alone] without [resorting to] boastful comparison with his neighbor.*

**GALATIANS 6:4**

I spent many years trying to be like other people. I tried to look like they looked, act like they acted, pray like they prayed, and do things they did. After much struggle, I finally realized God would never help me be anyone but myself. This is true for all of us. There is a reason He made us who we are and not like other people. Comparing ourselves to others and trying to be like they are complicates our lives. Nothing God has put within us is designed to copy someone else. It is much easier to simply be ourselves. God helps us do that because He wants us to express and enjoy the uniqueness of who He has created us to be.

You have no need or reason to compete or compare yourself with anyone else (2 Corinthians 10:12). Freedom from comparison and the liberty to be yourself is true freedom indeed. God does not compare us to anyone else. All He expects of us is that we try to be the best we can be. I often say, "God wants me to be the best me I can be." And He wants the same for you. Since I have realized this, I have grown considerably. Life has become more simple and more enjoyable. I believe the same will happen for you as you *simply express who you are.* God is honored when we thankfully embrace who He created us to be.

# REALIZE THAT MORE ISN'T ALWAYS BETTER

*Wealth [not earned but] won in haste or unjustly or from the production of things for vain or detrimental use [such riches] will dwindle away, but he who gathers little by little will increase [his riches].*

**PROVERBS 13:11**

Society often tells us that having more or doing more is better than having or doing less. I've found that this isn't necessarily true. The more possessions we have, the more cluttered our environment is, and the more commitments we make, the more complicated life becomes. Sometimes, more is not better at all; it's actually worse. I have learned to choose quality over quantity, and this has helped me greatly. Everything we own is something we must take care of; always remember that when you think of adding another possession to what you already have.

Think about this example. People often buy cheap clothes because they want to have more clothes. Then they feel frustrated or disappointed when the inexpensive items stretch easily, shrink, fade, pill, or don't look good after they've been laundered once or twice. Having better-quality clothes typically benefits us in the long run. We don't have to replace them as often, and we don't have so many choices when deciding what to wear. Perhaps you are like I am and would rather spend a certain amount on one piece of quality clothing that will hold up well and look good over time than to spend the same amount on two or three pieces that have to

9

be replaced quickly. The same is true for appliances, cars, accessories, and other items we use every day.

*I encourage you to develop the habit of buying the best quality you can afford, given your budget.* Resist the temptation to think that more is better because usually it isn't.

# COMMIT TO CROSS THE FINISH LINE

*I press on toward the goal to win the prize for which God has called me heavenward in Christ Jesus.*                    **PHILIPPIANS 3:14** NIV

Have you ever known anyone who approaches new projects and opportunities with seemingly unlimited energy but then loses interest and fails to follow through on their commitment? Many people are this way. They start things with great enthusiasm, but they don't finish. They either leave the project for someone else to complete, or it just remains undone.

New things can be exciting, but when the newness wears off, there's still work to be done or a commitment to be fulfilled. People who see their commitments through to the end are typically the ones who realistically assess the task at the beginning, thinking through what it requires in terms of time, energy, and other resources. They know the excitement won't last and are willing to do what it takes to get the project across the finish line.

Our society applauds multitasking and productivity, and because of this, people often take on more than they can reasonably handle. Then life becomes complicated, and other areas of their life suffer because they don't have time to give them the attention or effort they need.

*When you commit to something, be diligent in doing it well and finishing it.* Once you complete it, you will be satisfied in your soul because you'll know you have done the right thing. Your mind will be uncluttered, and you'll be free to move on to new dreams, new projects, new ideas, and new goals.

# KEEP THINGS IN PERSPECTIVE

*A person's wisdom yields patience; it is to one's glory to overlook an offense.*

**PROVERBS 19:11** NIV

Many people insist on worrying about the little problems in life, especially things like being offended by what other people say or do. We need to realize that no one says or does everything perfectly all the time, and there's no need to make a big deal out of things we could easily ignore. We can choose to stay at peace.

Life offers us many opportunities to be offended, but we can choose to let go of anything that makes no difference in the overall scope of life. The enemy will try to upset us, but we can remain at peace. Song of Solomon 2:15 says the "little foxes" spoil the vine, meaning that little things can cause big trouble. How many couples divorce over the small things they refuse to forget, which then grow into big problems? If we don't keep a record of wrongs (1 Corinthians 13:5), we will enjoy better, simpler relationships. I used to be a good "accountant" of offenses against me. Because I kept track of them and dwelled on them, my life was a complicated mess, and I was not happy.

Learn not to be easily offended, or you will forfeit your peace and your joy. *Remember that most people don't offend you on purpose.* Purify your thoughts and emotions by letting go of past offenses. Refuse to lose your peace and joy by meditating on what people have done *to* you. Instead, think about what people have done *for* you. Your life will become much simpler when you become willing to quickly and frequently forgive.

# GET YOUR MIND OFF YOURSELF

*Even to your old age and gray hairs I am he, I am he who will sustain you. I have made you and I will carry you; I will sustain you and I will rescue you.*

**ISAIAH 46:4** NIV

A self-centered life is complicated. God never intended us to focus too intensely on ourselves. He wants us to help others and to trust Him to take care of us.

If we want to simplify our lives, we need to stop thinking so much about ourselves and our own interests (Mark 8:34). Sometimes we think if we turn everything over to God, we won't enjoy life or have anything we want, but the opposite is true. When we give our lives away to others and trust God to do what needs to be done for us, He gives us a life beyond anything we could provide for ourselves.

Of course, we should take care of ourselves physically, mentally, emotionally, and spiritually. But we need to stop worrying about how we can get everything we want out of life. The more we think about ourselves, the more unhappy we will be.

Human nature fights for self-preservation, but when we accept Christ as Savior and Lord, we receive a new nature (2 Corinthians 5:17). This gives us the ability to be self*less*. We can learn a new way of living that says "It's no longer about me." Always trying to make sure we are taken care of is complicated, but trusting that God will care for us as we care for others is simple. *Let me encourage you to get your mind off yourself and choose to trust God, starting today.*

## DAY 13

# DON'T PUT THINGS OFF

*Again He sets a definite day, [a new] Today, [and gives another opportunity of securing that rest] saying through David after so long a time in the words already quoted, Today, if you would hear His voice and when you hear it, do not harden your hearts.*

**HEBREWS 4:7**

Life feels complicated when I have a dozen projects to finish and don't feel I have time for them all. I cannot enter God's rest until I listen to His direction and take action. Good intentions don't equal obedience.

Procrastination is one of the devil's great deceptions. How many unfinished tasks aggravate or even torment you? Think of the closet you intend to clean or those household repairs or phone calls you keep putting off. Just thinking about them can make you feel frustrated and disorganized and prevent you from enjoying life. The simple way to deal with such things is to set a day and time, and just get them done. One act of discipline will protect you from many days of feeling overwhelmed.

*If you have several unfinished tasks, don't get stressed and feel defeated before you begin them. Keep working at them one at a time.* Look at the finish line—and be determined to do what it takes to get there. You will have to discipline yourself and make sacrifices, but the reward will be freedom and enjoyment. The Bible says that no discipline seems pleasant at the time, but later it "yields a peaceable fruit of righteousness to those who have been trained by it" (Hebrews 12:11).

Discover the joy of an uncluttered life by deciding to be a "now" person who doesn't procrastinate, and you will experience the peace that comes from doing what you need to do when it needs to be done instead of putting it off.

# UNCLUTTER YOUR SURROUNDINGS

*For God is not a God of disorder but of peace.*

1 CORINTHIANS 14:33 NIV

Clutter overwhelms me. My husband, Dave, tends to hang on to things, but I like to clear out items I don't use or need. God gives us bread to eat and seed to sow (2 Corinthians 9:10), meaning that some things are intended to be passed on to others. I regularly give things away. I don't want to own so much that I can't enjoy what I have because everything appears untidy and disorderly.

One reason many people can't let go of clutter is that they feel guilty getting rid of gifts they've been given. They don't want to hurt the giver's feelings. But gifts given in the right spirit have no strings attached and are ours to do with as we please.

People sometimes give us gifts *they* like that don't suit our taste. We should not feel obligated to use these things. I once gave a friend an expensive bracelet, which I later noticed on another friend's arm. I was tempted to be hurt, but I remembered I had given it freely with no right to dictate what she did with it. Maybe giving it away was a sacrifice for my friend, and she did so in obedience to God but didn't really want to.

*If you struggle to get rid of clutter, consider starting a box with items someone else will like but you will never miss.* Free yourself from the complication of clutter, and enjoy peace and order in your life.

# KNOW WHEN ENOUGH IS ENOUGH

*Be well balanced (temperate, sober of mind), be vigilant and cautious at all times; for that enemy of yours, the devil, roams around like a lion roaring [in fierce hunger], seeking someone to seize upon and devour.*

1 PETER 5:8

When we become excessive in anything and don't recognize when enough is enough, we are no longer living a balanced life. This opens the door for the devil, who wants to steal our joy and push us toward excess. Having anything beyond our capacity to use it complicates our life and causes problems. So do excessive talking, excessive eating, excessive debt, and other excesses. Excess is the devil's playground.

The Bible talks about the necessity of pruning (Isaiah 18:5), the cutting off of excessive or diseased branches. Once Dave had one of our trees pruned. It was cut back so far, it looked horrible, and I was sure he had killed it. He said if I was patient, it would be prettier than ever the next spring. Sure enough, it turned out to be the most attractive tree in our yard.

Don't be afraid to cut back what you don't need. I believe such pruning opens the door for God to give you even more. *If you have more possessions than you can use, share them with someone who doesn't have enough.* This way, you will plant seeds for a future harvest in your own life. If some of the things you say cause trouble in your relationships, talk less and listen more. Say no to excess and yes to removing the complexity from your life today.

# LIVE DEBT-FREE

*The rich rule over the poor, and the borrower is servant to the lender.*
**PROVERBS 22:7**

Financial debt creates a complicated chokehold on our lives and puts a tremendous burden on marriages and families. Our society makes it easy to get into debt by using credit to buy now and pay later. We have become impatient, living for the moment, and caring little about the future. We purchase things in the height of emotion and then experience the pain of paying off the debt for months or years. This complicates our lives and steals the simplicity God wants us to enjoy.

I encourage you to buy what you need and learn to save for what you want, but don't go into debt to do it. The Bible says, "He who gathers little by little will increase [his riches]" (Proverbs 13:11). My husband has a simple plan: *Out of everything you get, give some, save some, and spend some within your borders or according to your ability.* Do this, and your borders (ability) will increase. You will not struggle with the stress and complication of debt.

If you are in debt, commit to get out of it. Don't keep doing the same things that got you into it. You may have to sacrifice to pay off the bills, but it will be worth it. Debt is like an iron weight you carry everywhere you go. Cut the ties, and feel the freedom and simplicity that comes with not owing anyone anything.

# MAJOR IN THE MAJORS

*Little children, keep yourselves from idols (false gods)—[from anything and everything that would occupy the place in your heart due to God, from any sort of substitute for Him that would take first place in your life]. Amen (so let it be).*

1 JOHN 5:21

If we want things to go well in our lives, we need to strive to keep God in first place. I use the word *strive* because if we put no effort into it, it never happens. Busyness can get our priorities out of line and cause us to put our energies into things that aren't truly important.

When Jesus visited Mary and Martha, they each responded to Him in different ways. Mary sat down at the Lord's feet to listen to Him, but Martha stayed busy cleaning and cooking. Jesus told Martha that Mary had made the better choice (Luke 10:38–42). Martha's life then became frustrating and complicated, while Mary's remained peaceful and serene because she understood what was most important. Martha needed to take advantage of the opportunity to hear Jesus teach while she could. There would be time to do the other things later.

Another time, Jesus met a rich young ruler who wanted to know how to experience eternal salvation. When Jesus told him to sell all he had, give it to the poor, and follow Him, the man went away sad because he had so many possessions (Luke 18:18–23). God was testing him. Had he been willing to give them up for God, he could have been given more than he had given away. Many people make this same mistake, fearfully clinging to what they have and losing what they could have. They accept things that can never satisfy as Jesus can. *Decide to keep first things first and major in the major things in life.* Jesus is the most important.

# DISCOVER THE BENEFITS OF BOUNDARIES

*From one man he made all the nations, that they should inhabit the whole earth; and he marked out their appointed times in history and the boundaries of their lands.*

**ACTS 17:26** NIV

God sets boundaries, and we should too. Without them, we have no protection. Like fences, they keep undesirable people and things out of our lives. Many people are afraid to set boundaries because they think they will offend someone. But God calls us to follow Him and walk in wisdom, not to let other people dictate what we must do to keep them happy.

Each person is different, so we need to respect their boundaries. For example, my younger daughter is strict about her privacy, so she asks people not to visit her without calling first. Our older daughter is just the opposite. We may not always understand why people are the way they are, but we need to honor their right to be themselves.

Without boundaries, life becomes frustrating and complicated. With no restraints or guidelines, we will feel taken advantage of. We may also end up in places we don't want to be, doing things we don't want to do.

We even need boundaries for ourselves, such as setting high standards to live by and deciding what we will and will not do. Saying no is setting a boundary.

To have no boundaries and not to respect the boundaries

21

of other people is not only foolish; it causes people to miss the simplicity they could enjoy. *Ask yourself what you need to be happy, and then set your boundaries accordingly.* This isn't wrong; it's wise, and it will help tremendously as you unclutter your life.

# KNOW WHO YOU ARE

*Jesus knew that the Father had put all things under his power, and that he had come from God and was returning to God.*

JOHN 13:3 NIV

I believe Jesus was able to do the humble act of washing His disciples' feet (John 13:1–17) because He knew Himself—who He was, where He came from, where He was going, and why He was sent.

Many people do not know who they are. They try to do things they have not been called or equipped to do. We should know not only what we *can* do, but what we *can't* do. One of the greatest tragedies I have witnessed as an employer is watching people remain in positions that either do not challenge them or are over their heads—yet they won't admit it.

Why do we have such a difficult time saying "That's not my strength, and I don't think I would do a good job at it"? We get too much of our value from what we do, instead of from who we are in Christ, which is all the position and title we will ever need.

The apostle Peter did not know himself. He had weaknesses he was not willing to admit. He thought he would never deny Christ, yet he did (Luke 22:54–62). After he repented, he was restored and became a great leader in the early church. Having weaknesses and inabilities doesn't disqualify us, because God's strength is made perfect in our weaknesses (2 Corinthians 12:9).

*Do all God calls and equips you to do, but don't try to go beyond what He has enabled you and given you grace to do.*

23

# HAVE FAITH

*Now faith is confidence in what we hope for and assurance about
what we do not see. This is what the ancients were commended for.*

**HEBREWS 11:1–2** NIV

Having faith in God is one of the best ways to simplify life.
Fear, doubt, unbelief, and overthinking complicate life, but
the ability to believe removes all of these. As Mark 5:36 says,
"only believe" (NKJV).

Sometimes our faith is challenged by the enemy or by
our circumstances. There's no such thing as a "belief button" to push to ensure we will never doubt again. When we
feel frustrated, instead of giving up, we need to realize that
we receive God's promises by faith and patience (Hebrews
6:12).

Negative emotions complicate our lives. We don't have
to get upset while we are waiting for God to move on our
behalf. We can choose to remain expectant and joyful. We
can simply believe.

*The next time you feel life is too cluttered and compli-
cated, say aloud, "I believe, God!"* Then remember the many
promises in His Word that assure us He will never leave us
or forsake us (Deuteronomy 31:6; Joshua 1:5; Hebrews
13:5–6). He is the source of every comfort and encourage-
ment (2 Corinthians 1:3–4). The more we focus on God's
promises, the less our problems bother us.

Faith in God has an amazing effect on the soul and brings
joy and peace (Romans 15:13). Any time I feel upset or sad,

I check my belief levels, and I can usually find the source of my negative emotion. If I am willing to adjust my attitude and increase my faith, things get better.

Only believe.

# ASSESS THE WAYS YOU SPEND YOUR TIME

*Look carefully then how you walk! Live purposefully and worthily and accurately, not as the unwise and witless, but as wise (sensible, intelligent people), making the very most of the time [buying up each opportunity], because the days are evil.*

EPHESIANS 5:15–16

Life rarely stays the same. Things always seem to shift and change. In order to grow, we must change also. As we seek to simplify our lives, we are wise to regularly assess our commitments and the ways we spend our time. Often, we get stuck in our routines without thinking much about what we are doing, and this can complicate our lives and clutter our calendars, because we may be doing something that no longer bears good fruit.

I believe we sometimes forfeit blessings God wants to give us because we fail to evaluate how we spend our time and to discontinue the things we no longer need to be doing. The fact that we have done certain things for many years doesn't mean we should keep doing them for years to come. God calls us to do some things for a season, and when the season is over, we need to stop doing them and find out what He wants us to do next.

Cutting activities we don't enjoy out of our schedules is easy. But sometimes in the process of maturity, God asks us to give up something we do enjoy. When this happens, we should remember that His plan is always best. He doesn't ask us to do things that won't make our lives better.

*I encourage you to regularly evaluate your commitments.* Do everything you feel God is asking and empowering you to do, and let go of things that are no longer effective. Ask Him to show you where you can make adjustments that will help you experience the joy of an uncluttered life.

# SET YOUR PRIORITIES

*Teach us to number our days, that we may gain a heart of wisdom.*
**PSALM 90:12** NIV

I believe people who are wise choose to do now what they will be happy with later. One way we can live wisely is to define our personal priorities and stick to them. For example, if a person makes a priority of being able to retire at age fifty-five, he or she will likely need to prioritize saving, investing, and wise stewardship of finances. When we clearly identify our priorities and live according to them, we simplify our lives because we remove many distractions and options. We know what we need to do to keep first things first.

If you need to begin to define your priorities, it's important to remember that what someone else does may not be right for you. *Let the Holy Spirit lead you to live your own life,* and be willing to be different if that's what it takes to live a simple, peaceful, wise, fulfilling life.

Many things compete for our attention, and when our priorities are clear, we know which ones to address first, second, and so on. Our first priority should be our personal relationship with God. If we allow anything to take priority over our walk with Him, life quickly becomes complicated and difficult. But when we start with Him and ask Him to lead us in setting subsequent priorities, He helps us live the good life He desires for us and has planned for us.

# CHOOSE YOUR BATTLES

*You will not have to fight this battle. Take up your positions; stand firm and see the deliverance the Lord will give you, Judah and Jerusalem. Do not be afraid; do not be discouraged. Go out to face them tomorrow, and the Lord will be with you.*

**2 CHRONICLES 20:17 NIV**

Sometimes living a simple, uncluttered life seems impossible because of the challenges we face in life. We do encounter trials and difficulties, but we don't have to let them complicate our lives unnecessarily by trying to deal with all of them. We can choose our battles, giving our time and energy to the ones we feel are worth the effort.

The longer we live, the more we realize that everything doesn't need to be addressed. Some things work themselves out without our intervention, and some situations are better off left alone. We can choose to deal with some circumstances by simply praying about them, never saying a word to anyone involved. In addition, the passing of time has a way of resolving situations. If we simply wait, we may be able to avoid certain types of battles altogether.

I have learned that unless something is truly urgent or some kind of emergency, it's rarely necessary for me to respond immediately. I often give myself a day or two to think about things and take time to weigh my options so I can make wise, solid decisions. I would encourage you to consider this approach, too. Realize that just because a problem comes your way, it doesn't mean you must deal with it immediately. You may not need to deal with it at all. *Choose to fight the battles that really matter.*

# PRACTICE FAST FORGIVENESS

*For if you forgive other people when they sin against you, your heavenly Father will also forgive you.*

MATTHEW 6:14 NIV

One of the ways people complicate their lives is by being easily offended and holding grudges. On the contrary, learning to forgive as soon as we've been hurt or wronged brings simplicity to our lives. In James 1:19, God's Word teaches us to be quick to forgive for a reason. He wants us to live in peace and joy, and this is impossible if we are bitter, resentful, and angry. As an old saying goes, refusing to forgive is like drinking poison and hoping it hurts the person who wronged you.

I have decided—and I hope you have, too—that I want to enjoy my life. But life is difficult to enjoy when we are angry or offended. When we linger in feelings of hurt or desire to seek revenge on someone, it affects our lives in negative ways. *I encourage you to set a goal right now that you will forgive people as fast as they hurt you.* The sooner you forgive people, the quicker the peace and joy return to your life.

Forgiveness is a choice, not a feeling. You may truly forgive someone and realize that your feelings toward that person have not changed. They may not change immediately, but as you continue to pray for them and treat them well, your feelings will eventually catch up to the godly choice you have made.

# KEEP YOUR OPINIONS TO YOURSELF

*Whoever guards his mouth and tongue keeps his soul from troubles.*
**PROVERBS 21:23** NKJV

God's Word is filled with practical advice for everyday life. One thing it instructs us to do is to mind our own business (1 Thessalonians 4:11). One of the primary ways we mind our own business is to avoid interfering in other people's lives by keeping our opinions to ourselves. Often, expressing an opinion or making comments about people or situations leads to relational problems and tends to keep life tense instead of peaceful.

Each of us has enough to think about without getting involved in other people's situations. If you have a tendency to meddle, give unsolicited advice, or inject your opinion when no one has asked for it, decide to stop doing that and *simply pray that God will lead the people around you and help them make good decisions.* Then refrain from commenting on what they decided to do or say.

I have had to tell myself many times, "Joyce, that is none of your business." This is often true for almost all of us. We like to know what's going on, and we may want people to know what we think about it, but we can keep life simple and peaceful if we learn to keep our opinions to ourselves. We often think, *I'm just trying to help*, but unless people want our help, they won't receive it, and offering our opinions could harm our relationship with them.

# SHOW MERCY AND KINDNESS

*Those who are kind benefit themselves, but the cruel bring ruin on themselves.*

**PROVERBS 11:17** NIV

A good way to simplify your life is to show mercy and kindness to those around you. I say this because everyone is imperfect. We all make mistakes, and at times we hurt or offend others. If we don't learn to be merciful, we may find ourselves irritated, frustrated, upset, or angry often. But we can choose to be peaceful by simply extending mercy to people.

Colossians 3:12 teaches us to treat others with "tenderhearted pity and mercy." To show mercy is to express compassion and heartfelt concern for other people. This doesn't come easily to everyone, but it is important for us to learn to do in relationships. When we make an effort to be merciful, we not only please God, we also save ourselves a lot of stress and turmoil.

Because of God's mercy, we are not consumed by our sin (Lamentations 3:22). He is merciful to us, and He expects us in turn to be merciful to others (Luke 6:36). Showing mercy to someone we feel deserves judgment or punishment instead may not seem fair from the world's perspective, but it is God's way. His ways are best for us. They are simple and peaceful, and they always bring a reward. *Remember that if you sow mercy, you will reap mercy when you need it* (Matthew 5:7).

# RESIST PASSING JUDGMENT

*"Do not judge, or you too will be judged. For in the same way you judge others, you will be judged, and with the measure you use, it will be measured to you."*

**MATTHEW 7:1–2** NIV

We may be tempted to pass judgment on what other people say and do, but only God has the right to judge anyone. I once heard that when we judge other people, we set ourselves up as God. This sounds like a dangerous and prideful thing to do.

It is easy to see or hear about certain circumstances and jump to conclusions about the situation or someone involved in it. Only God knows what someone is really doing, and only He knows why they are doing it and what is in their heart. We judge based on what we observe outwardly, but God looks inside people and sees their motives and their heart.

Each time we judge another person, we sow a seed that will lead to a harvest in our lives (Matthew 7:1). If we are critical and merciless, we can expect others to criticize us and withhold mercy from us. But if we are gracious and merciful toward others, we can expect people to be gracious and merciful to us.

Being judgmental is a symptom of pride. Proverbs 18:12 teaches us that pride comes before a person's downfall or destruction, but that humility precedes honor. When we pass judgment, things don't go well for us. *Be sure to view people with humility and refuse to judge them, so you will reap honor.*

33

# JUST DECIDE

*If any of you lacks wisdom, you should ask God, who gives
generously to all without finding fault, and it will be given to you. But
when you ask, you must believe and not doubt, because the one
who doubts is like a wave of the sea, blown and tossed by the wind.*

**JAMES 1:5–6** NIV

Confusion and indecision can make life very complicated
and make people feel tossed about by the wind. People can be
stressed for days when faced with certain decisions, but simplicity prays, seeks wisdom, and decides what to do. When we seek
God and know what He is leading us to do, there is no waffling.
We can confidently stick with a decision, even if acting on it
will not be easy, unless there is a compelling reason to change it.

*When you need to make a decision, do the best you can do
to seek wisdom and follow the leading of the Holy Spirit.* Don't
let the fear of making a mistake paralyze you by holding you
in indecision. Trust God to cover you and work things out
if you make a decision that later seems to be a mistake. He
looks at the heart (1 Samuel 16:7), and He doesn't expect us
to do more than the best we can do.

As you make decisions over the course of your life, you will
gain experience. Sometimes you'll see that what you did was
beneficial; other times you will learn not to do in the future
the same types of things you have done in the past. Each decision, in a way, is a practice round for future choices.

God loves you. He is merciful and gracious. Commit
today to unclutter your life by becoming a decisive person,
trusting Him to guide you to make great decisions and to
help you if you don't.

DAY
29

# THINK FIRST, THEN SPEAK

*Let your conversation be always full of grace, seasoned with salt, so that you may know how to answer everyone.*

COLOSSIANS 4:6 NIV

I don't know about you, but I have complicated many situations in the past simply because I said something before thinking it through. Over the years, I have grown in my ability to think before I speak and made lots of progress in this area, but I still make mistakes at times and have to remind myself to think and *then* speak.

According to James 3:8, "No human being can tame the tongue. It is a restless evil, full of deadly poison" (NIV). Our words can be the source of many problems, and even a few words, spoken recklessly, can cause much trouble. As James teaches us, we cannot tame our tongues in our own strength. But with God's help, we can learn to control the words we speak.

Words are containers for power. As James teaches, they can have great negative power. But they can also deliver positive power. Proverbs 18:21 says, "*Death and life* are in the power of the tongue, and those who love it will eat its fruit" (NKJV, italics mine). This is a strong statement, and we should take it seriously, realizing that we can do great damage—but also bring great blessing—through the words we speak. *I continue to ask God regularly to help me think before I speak and to use my words for life and not death, and I encourage you to do the same.*

35

# PRIORITIZE PLEASING GOD

*That you may walk worthy of the Lord, fully pleasing Him, being fruitful in every good work and increasing in the knowledge of God.*
**COLOSSIANS 1:10** NKJV

We can all be tempted to please other people because we want them to accept us. Wanting acceptance and not wanting to be rejected is normal. But when we give in to the pressure to please people instead of God, we allow them to control us instead of letting Him lead us. This will keep us from fulfilling our God-ordained destiny.

For years, I tried to avoid rejection by trying to please people and, therefore, allowing them to control me. Eventually, I discovered they were much more interested in getting what they thought was best for them than helping me do what was best for me. They were using me to make them happy but had no desire to see me happy, too. When God called me into ministry, the people I thought were my friends almost immediately rejected me. I felt deeply hurt, but I am grateful that God helped me choose Him over them.

I thank God that I no longer live a life of pretense, trying to win the favor of people who did not genuinely care about me. *Understand that your true friends will be sincerely interested in you, want the best for you, and do all they can do to help you become all God wants you to be.* They will encourage you to please Him, not them.

# RESIST GUILT AND CONDEMNATION

*Therefore, there is now no condemnation for those who are in Christ Jesus.*

**ROMANS 8:1** NIV

Guilt is a feeling that we have done something wrong, and we feel bad about it. Condemnation is a feeling of heaviness and shame that weighs on us and seems to press us down. This is why some people say they are "under" condemnation.

Jesus came to lift us up, not to press us down. It is our enemy, the devil, who wants to keep us feeling down and depressed. He brings condemnation, but Jesus offers us forgiveness and restoration. The enemy brings complexity and confusion, but Jesus offers simplicity. When we sin, the Holy Spirit convicts us, but the enemy tries to condemn us. We need to know the difference between conviction and condemnation. Conviction leads us to admit our sin and repent. Then we can receive God's forgiveness. Condemnation only makes us feel guilty and "wrong." It keeps us from asking for and receiving the forgiveness that sets us free.

*Decide today not to accept feelings of guilt and condemnation.* Remember that Jesus paid the price for our sins by dying on the cross and rising from the dead. If we look to Him as our Savior, we are free from the power of sin (Romans 6:7–8), which I believe includes guilt and condemnation. We can't enjoy a simple life if we succumb to guilt and condemnation every time we fail. Thank God, Jesus Christ offers us a life filled with peace and joy as we resist guilt and condemnation.

## DAY 32    DON'T LET FEAR CONTROL YOU

*The Lord is my Light and my Salvation—whom shall I fear or dread? The Lord is the Refuge and Stronghold of my life—of whom shall I be afraid?*

**PSALM 27:1**

Fear can make life complicated and difficult. Satan uses the torment of fear to keep us out of God's will and hinder us as we try to move forward in life. People fear a lot of things. The truth is, someone is afraid of just about anything you can think of.

Though we may feel fear, we do not have to give in to it. We can still do what's necessary, even if we have to "do it afraid." Courage is not the absence of fear but taking action in the presence of fear.

When God leads us to do something, He supplies everything we need to do it—ability, help, finances, courage, and wisdom. We may not see these provisions immediately, but as we step out in faith, they will be there. Satan uses fear to make us shrink back from what we want to do and feel God is leading us to do, but God wants us to follow through and fulfill our dreams.

We cannot win our battles when we give in to fear. Gideon was headed to war, and God told him to dismiss all the fearful soldiers, close to two-thirds of them (Judges 7:3). We don't need to reject people who experience fear, but we should not allow those who are controlled by it to influence us.

*Say no to fear.* It complicates, confuses, and causes us to act irrationally. God has not given us a spirit of fear, but of power, love, and a sound mind (2 Timothy 1:7).

38

# LISTEN TO YOUR HEART

*For we are God's handiwork, created in Christ Jesus to do good works, which God prepared in advance for us to do.*

EPHESIANS 2:10 NIV

We can complicate and clutter our lives by ignoring what is important to us. When we put aside what is in our hearts and follow what other people think we should do, we end up empty and unfulfilled. We go through the motions, but nothing satisfies us. We spend so much time meeting our obligations that we forget what *we* want.

*Ask yourself, "What do I want out of life?"* I'm not talking about pursuing selfish interests or sinful behavior, but the desires God has planted in your heart. Everyone is called and equipped to do something, including you. It takes boldness to follow your heart instead of the crowd. When God called me to teach His Word, it was not popular for women to do that. I lost friends, and some of my family members rejected me as a rebel, viewing me as deceived and misguided. But over time, God has redeemed all of that and blessed me more than I ever dreamed possible.

Ignoring your dreams while forcing yourself to do something you don't enjoy makes life complicated, not simple. You may think following your heart will complicate your life if certain people don't like it or no longer accept you, but it's the only way to enjoy a simple life of obedience to God.

# DON'T FEAR OTHER PEOPLE'S OPINIONS

*Am I now trying to win the approval of human beings, or of God? Or am I trying to please people? If I were still trying to please people, I would not be a servant of Christ.*

**GALATIANS 1:10** NIV

Being excessively concerned about what other people think sets us up for torment. We all enjoy being well thought of, but it is not realistic to expect everyone to be like we are or approve of everything we do.

First Peter 5:7 tells us to cast all our cares on God because He cares for us. This includes caring what people think. I can only live to please God, and if people are not satisfied with that, then they will have to take it up with Him, not me. If I try to please both God and people, life gets complicated, and I get confused and frustrated.

When I first decided to please God, I experienced rejection from friends. Later, God gave me new friends who were pursuing Him as I was. I learned that we often have to be willing to lose something we have in order to gain what we really want.

Why hang on to something that will never satisfy you? Don't live under the tyranny of other people's opinions. *Stop trying to convince other people of your good intentions, and let them think what they want to think.* God is your defender. He will vindicate you in due time.

What can someone's thoughts do to you anyway? God

has not given us His Holy Spirit so we can be held captive by fear (Romans 8:15). Decide to care more about what God thinks than what anyone else thinks, and it will simplify your life.

# LIVE LIFE WITHOUT STRIFE

*It is to one's honor to avoid strife, but every fool is quick to quarrel.*
**PROVERBS 20:3** NIV

Strife is the bickering, arguing, heated disagreement, and angry undercurrent we sometimes experience in relationships. Second Timothy 2:23–24 says that those who serve God must not get caught up in strife. We are to be diligent in avoiding "foolish and stupid arguments" because "they produce quarrels" and lead to strife (v. 23 NIV).

To keep conflict and discord out of our lives, we need to avoid conversations that lead to distress and turmoil. When Dave and I are having a conversation that becomes intense, we often choose to just drop it because what we are debating is not worth arguing about. We are determined to keep strife out of our life.

One reason strife often arises is that people want to be right. But if we want to live in peace, we should consider that even though we think we are right, there is a possibility we are wrong. We can cause all kinds of problems trying to prove our points. In the end, being right is highly overrated, and it does nothing but satisfy the flesh.

The anger and arguing involved in strife make life feel really complicated. But God has called us to peace (1 Corinthians 7:15). Strife weakens us, blocks our blessings, and opens the door for trouble. But agreement increases our power.

*The next time you sense strife threatening a relationship, stop and ask yourself if what you're debating is worth losing your peace over.* Do all you can to live a peaceful life.

## DAY 36

# BECOME AN OPTIMIST

*Be constantly renewed in the spirit of your mind [having a fresh mental and spiritual attitude].*

**EPHESIANS 4:23**

Being positive is a choice, and a positive attitude opens a door for God to work in our lives. But we can also choose to be negative and open a door for the devil. Even if you are in an unpleasant situation, being negative won't change it. We are wise to ask ourselves, "Is my problem *really* my problem, or is my real problem the way I view my problem?"

Once we allow negativity to slant our viewpoint and become the filter through which we see life, we lose our joy and peace. People who are negative have trouble getting answers from God, so they feel confused about what to do, and things go from bad to worse.

For many years, I was a very negative person. I was raised in a negative environment, so I didn't know how to be optimistic or hopeful. My life was not enjoyable, and it was anything but simple. My problems grew worse instead of better because I complained so much about them. Only when I started focusing on the positive and releasing the negative did God's peace begin to come into my world.

If you have a negative outlook, you can become optimistic by simply choosing to focus on the positive. God is waiting to answer a lot of your prayers, but He needs you to have an attitude of faith. *Remind yourself that being negative does no good.* Concentrate on the positive things in life, and you will be amazed at all the good you can find.

# FOCUS ON YOUR STRENGTHS

*For as we have many members in one body, but all the members
do not have the same function, so we, being many, are one body in
Christ, and individually members of one another.*

**ROMANS 12:4-5 NKJV**

Have you been trying and failing to keep up with the talents
and abilities of the successful people you know? If you want to
experience the joy of an uncluttered life, learn to give the major-
ity of your time to your top two or three strengths and stop
wasting it on things you don't do well. We are all encouraged by
accomplishment, so if we keep doing things that don't succeed,
we will always feel like a failure, and we won't enjoy our lives.

*You don't have to do something well just because some-
one you know does.* My previous neighbor was the perfect
homemaker—a great seamstress, gardener, decorator, and
cook. I could not sew, had no garden, and was an average
cook. I attempted a garden but hated it. I tried to sew but
hated that even more. Life was complicated and miserable because I did things I hated so I could feel like what I
thought was a "normal woman."

God had to teach me that the fact that I was not like my
neighbor did not mean something was wrong with me. I had
to stop doing things I did not do well and stop worrying
what people thought about me. If we were all good at the
same things, many needs in this world would not be met.
God equips each of us in a different way, and it is by working
together with our own individual strengths and talents that
we accomplish His will.

# TRUST GOD WITH THE ONES YOU LOVE

*Can any one of you by worrying add a single hour to your life?*
**MATTHEW 6:27** NIV

Some people feel that if they don't worry and fret about their children, they are not good parents. But the Bible teaches that worry is useless and not God's will, much like rocking in a rocking chair that keeps you busy but gets you nowhere.

*Do the best you can to raise your children according to godly principles, and leave the rest to God.* When we worry, we show that we don't really trust God. We need to pray for our loved ones and then cast our care on God (1 Peter 5:7).

I have four grown children who are all serving God now, but I wasted a lot of time worrying while they were growing up. I wondered if a couple of them could even survive if they left home. To my surprise, they have done very well.

If you have children, don't be afraid to let them spread their wings and fly solo at the right time. Some of my children took a little detour and made some bad choices, but they learned from them and came back full circle to what they were taught. Proverbs 22:6 says that if we train them in the way they should go, when they are old they will not depart from it.

Cling to this promise for your children. Worry only confuses and complicates your life. It won't help your children or anyone else you worry about, so put the energy you spend being anxious into believing God instead. Then watch Him work on your behalf.

# REIN IN YOUR REASONING

*Lean on, trust in, and be confident in the Lord with all your heart and mind and do not rely on your own insight or understanding.*

**PROVERBS 3:5**

God's Word teaches us not to rely on our own understanding. In other words, we don't need to waste time trying to figure out things only God knows. He invites us to simplify our lives by trusting Him, realizing that we will always have unanswered questions. If we knew everything, we wouldn't need God. Our job as believers is not to have all the answers but to trust God to provide them at the right time.

An important way I learned to simplify my life was to stop reasoning—analyzing and fretting over things, trying to come up with answers that made sense. I felt mentally worn out, and much of what I thought I figured out was wrong anyway. Once I decided to stop doing this, it took time for my flesh to settle down and feel peaceful. Whenever I started to feel confused, I knew I had slipped back into my old habit, and I would say aloud, "God, I trust You, and I refuse to get into reasoning." Gradually, I was delivered from "the need to know." I am now comfortable not knowing and not even trying to figure out most things because I know God, and He knows everything. I can rest in His love and know He is in control.

*If you often feel trapped in reasoning, I encourage you to ask God to set you free and learn to trust Him.* He understands everything.

# CHOOSE YOUR FRIENDS WISELY

*The righteous choose their friends carefully, but the way of the wicked leads them astray.*

**PROVERBS 12:26** NIV

The people we spend time with have a significant impact on us, so it stands to reason that if we want simple, uncluttered lives, we should have friends who live simple, uncluttered lives. We should not have a lot of complicated people as our close friends. If we are around people who are uptight and stressed, we may feel stressed too. If we are around people who are easygoing and peaceful, we tend to relax. And if we are around people who are lighthearted and who thoroughly enjoy the simple things in life, their influence reminds us to do likewise.

We need to choose our friends wisely and carefully. Some people make foolish choices simply because they become friends with someone they see often, such as a neighbor or coworker. But friends who are chosen just because they are convenient may also be complicated—not always, but possibly. People who base their friendships on convenience would be wise to rethink the type of people they spend time with.

I have had enough complexity in my life. I don't want to spend time with someone who seems to complicate every plan, every conversation, and every hour we spend together. Perhaps you feel the same way. *I encourage you to evaluate your friendships, and if some of them consistently make your life complicated instead of simple, consider making some adjustments.*

# BE EFFICIENT

*Behave yourselves wisely [living prudently and with discretion] in your relations with those of the outside world (the non-Christians), making the very most of the time and seizing (buying up) the opportunity.*
**COLOSSIANS 4:5**

When we waste our time, we are wasting one of the most precious gifts God gives us. Every moment that passes is one we will never get back, so we should use our time wisely and learn to be efficient.

One way you can learn to be efficient is to combine errands. Sometimes we feel good because we get things done without procrastinating, but when running errands, that's not always the best strategy. *Instead, try thinking about your errands so you can plan a route that doesn't waste time or gas, and set a convenient time to do what you need to do.* This will help you streamline the tasks before you and keep you from backtracking and feeling frazzled.

In recent years, technology has given us several tools to increase our efficiency. With just the click of a button on our computers or devices, we can now do some things that used to take several minutes. Whenever we can use technology as a time-saving device, and when we are comfortable doing so, we should consider it.

There are many ways to save time, and we would be wise to take a few minutes to think through how we can do it. Think about what you do regularly and what you have done recently, and see if you can come up with creative ways to be more efficient. This will help you greatly in your quest for a simple life.

# DEVELOP AN ATTITUDE
# OF GRATITUDE

*Praise the Lord. Give thanks to the Lord, for he is good; his love
endures forever.*

**PSALM 106:1** NIV

Being thankful and expressing our gratitude is not only good for
us; it helps simplify our lives. We can all find plenty to complain
about, and once we start complaining, we tend to think of more
and more negative situations. Philippians 2:14 tells us, "Do all
things without grumbling and faultfinding and complaining."
The antidote to complaining is an attitude of gratitude.

I once asked God for something, and He showed me that
I often complained about what I already had, so there was no
reason for Him to give me anything else. Since that time, I
have made an effort to be intentionally grateful. I even wrote
a book about it, called *The Power of Thank You.*

A thankful heart shows God that we are ready for a new level
of blessings. Gratitude to God is part of the lifestyle of people
who praise, worship, and honor Him. We don't live a lifestyle
of worship if we grumble and complain all week, then go to
church on Sunday and sing a few songs. That merely means we
have attended a worship service. I want to be a true worshipper
who gives God thanks and praise throughout each day, for He
is worthy of all the thanks and praise we can offer—and more.

*Develop an attitude of gratitude and watch how it will sim-
plify your life.* It will free your mind from complaints and
complicated thoughts, allowing you to be at peace and simply enjoy who God is and all He does for you.

# ASSESS WHAT YOU'LL NEED
# TO INVEST

*Suppose one of you wants to build a tower. Won't you first sit
down and estimate the cost to see if you have enough money to
complete it?*

LUKE 14:28 NIV

Most of the worthwhile things we do require an investment
of some sort—time, energy, thought, money, creativity, or
other resources. When good ideas or appealing opportunities come to us, we often get excited about them but fail to
think through the investments they will require. In other
words, we don't always count the cost of pursuing what we
want to do. Enthusiasm can turn to regret once we get over
the excitement of a new project and realize how much work
it will involve or how much time or money it will take. As I
often say, "Let emotions subside and then decide." *In other
words, give the emotional high of a new opportunity a chance to
level out so that before you agree to it you can realistically assess
the investment you'll need to make in it.*

People tend to complicate their lives by agreeing to do
too many things without considering what they will have to
sacrifice or how a new commitment will impact their already
busy schedules. We can all get caught up in the moment and
think we want to do something, especially if it sounds really
fun or if our friends are doing it. For example, a beach trip
with your best friends would be fun. But when you realize
it will cost almost as much as a necessary dental procedure
and you cannot afford to do both, you would hopefully see

the wisdom of taking care of your teeth instead of going on vacation.

Anyone can greatly simplify their life by considering the investments needed to do the things they think they want to do and deciding whether those investments will pay off in meaningful ways.

# COMMIT EVERYTHING TO PRAYER

*And pray in the Spirit on all occasions with all kinds of prayers and requests. With this in mind, be alert and always keep on praying for all the Lord's people.*

**EPHESIANS 6:18** NIV

The more we try to make our own decisions or do things in our own strength without asking God to help us, the more complicated life will be. We need His guidance, help, and blessing in everything we do, and we ask and receive these through prayer. First, we should ask Him to show us whether we need to do certain things and, if so, how to go about them. If He leads us to do them, we should depend on Him to help us. Too often, we make decisions apart from Him and jump into situations, and then we wonder why we struggle with them.

Jesus is the Author and Finisher of our faith (Hebrews 12:2 NKJV), but He is not obligated to finish anything He doesn't start. According to John 5:19, Jesus does "nothing by himself; he can do only what he sees his Father doing" (NIV). This is the example we should follow.

God's grace helps us do with ease what we could never do on our own with any amount of human strength or wisdom. *Whether you're going on a diet, starting a new career, getting married, or doing anything else, remember to pray about it.* Ask God to lead you, help you make good decisions, and enable you to do what you need to do. He will be faithful to answer.

# DON'T WORRY ABOUT WRONGDOERS

*Do not fret because of those who are evil or be envious of those who do wrong.*

**PSALM 37:1** NIV

We don't have to look far to see evidence of wrongdoing in our society. In 2 Timothy 3:1–9, Paul writes about the kind of people who will operate in the world during the last days. Among other things, he characterizes them as lovers of self, proud and contemptuous boasters, abusive, ungrateful, profane, morally loose, "haters of good" (v. 3), treacherous, and "inflated with self-conceit" (v. 4). I believe we are living in the times Paul writes about. We see the behavior he describes in many places in our culture. With all the troubles the world faces today, it would be easy to worry. But God tells us not to fret over those who do evil. Instead, according to Psalm 37:3, we are to trust in Him and do good.

Evil is not new. It happened in Jesus' day, and He certainly witnessed it. But instead of worrying about it, He focused on obeying God and doing good. God will take care of wrongdoers in due time (Psalm 37:2, 10). Sometimes it does appear that those who do wrong get away with it and fare better than those who don't. This is frustrating and confusing. But Psalm 37:34 says, "Hope in the Lord and keep his way. He will exalt you to inherit the land; when the wicked are destroyed, you will see it" (NIV).

When you see people doing wrong, don't worry; pray for them to see their evil ways. *Trust God and keep doing good.*

# DAY 46   PUT YOURSELF IN GOD'S HANDS

*But by the grace of God I am what I am, and His grace toward me was not in vain; but I labored more abundantly than they all, yet not I, but the grace of God which was with me.*

**1 CORINTHIANS 15:10 NKJV**

Do you ever struggle with certain things about yourself? Do you see things you know you need to change and desperately try to change them? Has trying to change yourself left you frustrated and tired? I tried for many years to change myself. Those were some of the most complicated years of my life. Eventually, God helped me see that trying to change myself was a waste of time and energy. By His grace, I realized that only He could change me.

When God shows us something that needs to change about ourselves, all He wants us to do is agree with Him and repent, if it is something we have truly done wrong. He will be faithful to do what needs to be done in our lives as we are honest with Him, admit that we can't change ourselves, ask for His help, obey what He leads us to do, and thank Him that He is working. We may not see immediate results, but when we put ourselves in His hands, results will come in due time.

If you have worn yourself out trying to do what only God can do in you, decide to trust Him instead, and let Him change you. *Stop wrestling with yourself, and believe that He is working in your life right now.* Every change He brings to your life will be a good one.

54

# LET GOD DEAL WITH OTHER PEOPLE

*But in fact God has placed the parts in the body, every one of them, just as he wanted them to be.*

1 CORINTHIANS 12:18 NIV

One mistake that really complicates our relationships and fills our lives with mental and emotional clutter is trying to make other people into who we want them to be instead of letting them be themselves. We often like people initially because they bring newness and variety to our lives, but eventually the fact that they are different may bother us. Then we try to make them more like we are. This doesn't work because God creates people differently on purpose. Just as every part of the human body can't be the head or the foot, in the body of Christ, every person has a different function, a different personality, and different traits—and we all need each other. Learn to love people the way they are, not the way you want them to be.

Many people are drawn to someone—perhaps as a friend or even as a spouse—who seems to be their complete opposite in many important ways. We tend to be attracted to people who complement (complete) us, not to people who copy us. They have what we lack. This can be wonderful until a problem arises in the relationship, and we forget what drew us to the person to begin with. That's when we start to try to change them.

Only God can change people, and only when they are

willing to be changed. If you want someone in your life to change, remember that you are powerless to do it. *Pray about the situation, and trust God to do what needs to be done in the other person's life,* while letting Him work in yours to make the changes He wants to make in you.

**DAY 48**

# MAKE A BIG CIRCLE

*Dear friends, since God so loved us, we also ought to love one
another.*

1 JOHN 4:11 NIV

God has called us to love everyone just as He loves us. He
doesn't reject anyone, and we shouldn't either. The world
is filled with lonely people. Some of them may be different
than we are or seem hard to understand, causing us to realize that we may need to make more effort than usual and be
intentional when extending friendship to them. Instead of
avoiding these people, we should be diligent in making our
circle of inclusion large and invite them into it.

I felt severely rejected for many years. I could sense that
people did not like me, and I didn't understand why. Some
even asked me, "Why do you act the way you do?" I had
no answer because I didn't know what bothered them about
me. I know now that because I was sexually abused by my
father, my personality became hard and harsh. I acted like I
didn't care about other people or need anyone, but inside I
was desperate for love and acceptance.

Only when I received God's unconditional love and
acceptance did I begin to heal. He wants you and me to love
and accept others, even when ignoring them seems easier.
First John 4:19 says that we can love others because God
loved us first.

*Always remember how much God loves you, and let that
inspire you to love others and include them in your circle of
friendship.*

57

# LET GOD TAKE IT

*Do not be anxious about anything, but in every situation, by prayer and petition, with thanksgiving, present your requests to God.*

**PHILIPPIANS 4:6** NIV

You may have been struggling with something at some time and a well-meaning person encouraged you to "just let God take it." This is often not the answer we want to hear when we are hurting, because what we really want is to fix the situation ourselves and move forward. But relinquishing our circumstances to God and letting Him handle them is the best thing we can do.

Letting go of the things we wrestle with and letting God take care of them requires faith. It isn't always easy, but it does make life easier because we are no longer trying to figure out what to do. We can relax, knowing that God is in control. I like to say "Do your best and let God do the rest."

Consider asking yourself what you may be trying to do that only God can do. What are you trying to bring about, solve, fix, or take care of that really is beyond your control? *I encourage you to stop right now and say aloud to God, "This is something I cannot make happen, Lord, and I release it to You right now."* Once you've done that, resist the temptation to take the situation back. You can cast all your burdens and anxieties on God because He cares for you (1 Peter 5:7), and He will always do what is best for you.

# MANAGE YOUR MIND

*You will keep him in perfect peace, whose mind is stayed on You, because he trusts in You.*

**ISAIAH 26:3** NKJV

When our thoughts are confused and complicated, everything else in our lives tends to become confused and complicated too. If we want our lives to change, we must first change our thoughts.

You can begin to change your life today by simply changing the way you think. Many people think whatever pops into their minds, but you don't have to be one of them. *You can choose to manage and discipline your mind to think positive thoughts, not negative thoughts, and to think in agreement with God's Word, not in opposition to it.*

The human mind is the battlefield on which Satan tries to plant thoughts in our minds to disrupt our relationship with God, make us think ungodly thoughts about ourselves, discourage us, and cause many other problems. He is a liar, and he hopes we will believe the lies he tells us. He knows that if he can control our minds, he can control us.

God's Word teaches us to "take captive every thought to make it obedient to Christ" (2 Corinthians 10:5 NIV). To do this, we need to know God's Word, because it teaches us truth. When we know the truth, we can resist lies. Managing your mind in accordance with God's Word may be a battle, but if you keep at it, you will win. God always leads us to victory (2 Corinthians 2:14).

# DAY 51 — UNCOMPLICATE YOUR LIFE

*The Lord preserves the simple; I was brought low, and He helped and saved me.*

**PSALM 116:6**

Are you like I once was—so determined to make things perfect and impressive that they turn into a nightmare rather than becoming the dream you envisioned? Being overly picky about nonessential details takes time and energy, and often we are the only people who notice them. The people we may try to impress don't really care, yet our drive for perfection keeps us from enjoying the simple life.

When Dave and I built our first home, I labored over decisions about faucets and doorknobs. One day much later, a friend asked me about my faucets because she was building a home, and I couldn't remember what they looked like. How sad is that? Dave and I have since built two other homes, and I have yet to see anyone stare at the faucets and doorknobs. If they are important to you, of course, take your time selecting them, but if they won't make much difference, get what looks good and move on.

Sometimes overthinking your options only leads to confusion and frustration. Most people, especially women, want to see all their options before making a decision, but then they end up getting something they saw three days and fourteen stores ago. *To simplify your life and save time, buy what you like when you see it. Don't keep looking for days in case you might see something better.*

Work at having a simple approach to everything you do. Life is too short to live it in frustration.

# ANTICIPATE IMPERFECTIONS

*Do everything without grumbling or arguing.*

**PHILIPPIANS 2:14** NIV

Unrealistic expectations can steal your peace and joy. Expecting a perfect day with perfect people in a perfect world isn't realistic. Only God is perfect; the rest of us are still works in progress.

The devil works hard to steal our peace and upset us. *Instead of panicking when things don't go exactly as planned, why not plan for some unexpected mishaps or delays?* In the last three days, I have broken a new dish, spilled water all over the floor, and dropped a coffee cup full of coffee. Of course, the cup broke, and glass and coffee were all over the floor—and it was only five o'clock in the morning.

Situations such as these used to upset me. I murmured and complained about how nothing ever worked out right. But my grumbling didn't stop these things from happening. In fact, my frustration caused me to lose focus, creating more accidents and mishaps. After years of letting the devil laugh at my fits, I finally realized that life is not perfect, and things I do not plan for are going to happen. My new attitude is "Oh well, I'll just clean that up."

Everyone must deal with inconveniences, but we need to stop acting in childish ways so that we can deal with them without a bad attitude. We need to grow up and have good attitudes when things don't go perfectly. This approach has greatly simplified my life. I no longer feel I have to get upset every day because everything doesn't go my way. And neither do you.

# BE PLEASANT AND EASYGOING

*Be of the same [agreeable] mind one with another; live in peace, and [then] the God of love [Who is the Source of affection, goodwill, love, and benevolence toward men] and the Author and Promoter of peace will be with you.*

2 CORINTHIANS 13:11

Most of us probably wish people were easier to get along with. But have we asked ourselves if we are easy to get along with?

How do you respond when you don't get your way? Are you easily offended? Do you need a lot of attention to feel good about yourself? How do you handle correction? Are you adaptable? Do you demand perfection from others? There was a time in my life when my answers to these questions would have been embarrassing.

I wanted everyone else to change so I could be happy, but God showed me that *I* was the problem. I was hard to please and easy to offend. I wanted my way, and I didn't act nice when I didn't get it. My attitude complicated my life because I spent a lot of time being upset.

Admitting that I was hard to get along with wasn't easy, but doing it opened a whole new way of life for me. I found that adapting to situations was sometimes easier than demanding my own way. I realized that if people did their best, I could compliment them instead of finding mistakes and correcting them. I learned I could simply let go of many things, and it would not make any difference in the overall outcome. With each petty thing I was able to give up, my life became a bit simpler.

*Ask yourself today if you are easy to get along with. If you need to improve in this area, ask God to help you.*

# THINK REALISTICALLY ABOUT YOURSELF

*Pride brings a person low, but the lowly in spirit gain honor.*

**PROVERBS 29:23** NIV

Nothing is wrong with believing in yourself. I don't think Jesus died for us so we could belittle and devalue ourselves. But the Bible does teach us not to think more highly of ourselves than we ought to, but to judge our abilities soberly, remembering the grace of God (Romans 12:3).

If we think too highly of ourselves, we will think too little of others. Remember, God gives us the ability to do what we do well. We should thank Him and never think less of someone else because their abilities are different than ours.

I consider myself an "everything-nothing" person: everything in Christ and nothing in myself. As Philippians 4:13 says, "I can do all things through Christ who strengthens me" (NKJV). And as Jesus says in John 15:5, "Apart from me you can do nothing" (NIV).

Having a humble view of ourselves and being willing to serve others, especially when they really need our help, is the simple approach to life. Jesus lived a simple, enjoyable life, yet His entire focus was on serving His heavenly Father and those He encountered each day. When we compare ourselves with the standards Jesus set for us, we have no reason to be full of pride.

People who are proud and judgmental or who look for faults in others will struggle in relationships. They won't succeed for long, because pride comes before destruction and a haughty spirit before a fall (Proverbs 16:18).

*Develop a proper attitude toward yourself* so you can begin to enjoy peace of mind. And when you have peace of mind, you can begin to enjoy life.

# MANAGE THE MAIL

*Avoid it...turn from it and pass on.*

PROVERBS 4:15

Most of us get all kinds of unwanted mail, both physically and electronically. I remember feeling guilty throwing paper mail away or deleting emails without reading them until God showed me that I'm not obligated to read what someone sends me unsolicited. If I do, I let them control my time and attention.

It is sad that we can look at a pile of mail or an inbox with lots of unsolicited messages and feel overwhelmed before we even start going through it. We can't keep people from sending it, but we don't have to keep it. *Recycle or throw away paper mail you don't want, and delete emails you don't need to respond to. Don't keep them just in case you ever have time to get around to reading them.* If a piece of mail or an electronic message isn't important enough to look at now, or in the next few days, chances are you'll never look at it.

At one point, I was about twenty issues behind in reading a particular magazine. I kept piling them up, planning to read them "someday." One day I got tired of looking at them and gave them away at the office. I do enjoy this magazine when time permits, but now I give it away when it comes unless I know I will soon have time to read it.

The only way to avoid having piles of stuff all over the house and a cluttered inbox is to systematically deal with mail and messages. When you have excess paper clutter, throw it away, recycle it, or give it away if it has value. If you have too many emails, hit the Delete button, but don't keep either physical or electronic mail or let it clutter your environment or your devices.

# MAKE YOUR PHONE WORK FOR YOU, NOT AGAINST YOU

*And he is drawn in diverging directions [his interests are divided and he is distracted from his devotion to God].*

1 CORINTHIANS 7:34

I remember when the only way to make a phone call when you were not at home was to find a pay phone and use it. Being able to carry a cell phone everywhere we go is convenient, but we should not let it control us. *If it rings at a time that isn't good for you to answer, then don't answer it, and return the call at a time when you can talk.* Do you ever get tired of answering the phone and hearing a preprogrammed message or a salesperson trying to sell you something you don't want or need?

You don't have to take every call that comes in on your phone. Technology today enables us to know who is calling most of the time, and it may be someone you can call back later when you have time. This way, you will manage your day instead of it managing you.

You can block phone numbers you don't recognize or callers you know you don't want to talk to.

Even if a call is one I want to take, I have learned that I don't have to take it immediately if it is not a good time for me. My days go much more smoothly if I set aside a certain amount of time to return calls instead of interrupting what I am doing to answer the phone every time it rings.

Learn to manage your phone, because this is one way you can simplify your life, increase your peace, and save some time.

# DON'T LET PROJECTS PILE UP

*Sluggards do not plow in season; so at harvest time they look but find nothing.*

**PROVERBS 20:4** NIV

Do you feel overwhelmed just looking at everything you need to do? A good way to simplify your life is not to let work pile up. When faced with a project you don't want to do, it's easy to decide to do it later. It takes willpower to stay with a task and not find excuses to leave the work unfinished.

You may have heard the saying "An idle mind is the devil's playground." When we allow ourselves to be idle, we can find many excuses to stay that way, such as "I need more time" or "I'm too tired" or "I don't have the capacity for that right now." Whatever excuses you make, if you were busy working, you wouldn't have time to come up with them, and the work wouldn't pile up.

Living a simple life requires self-control. It's important to decide what needs to be done and systematically do it without excuses. This may be challenging at first, especially if you haven't been disciplined in the past, but the rewards of order and restraint are worth the effort. The Bible says that discipline brings peaceable fruit (Hebrews 12:11).

*If you really believe you are supposed to do a certain task, decide not to put it off, unless you are faced with an emergency.* Just get the job done and do it to the best of your ability.

# PLAN FOR YOUR PRIORITIES

*The plans of the diligent lead surely to plenty, but those of everyone who is hasty, surely to poverty.*

**PROVERBS 21:5** NKJV

Years ago, I started working with a nutritionist and personal trainer so I could have optimal health and energy in the future. He said, "It will be impossible for you to do this if you don't plan ahead." Now, I intentionally plan to go to certain food stores so I have the right foods to eat. It's easy to make wrong choices if we don't have healthy options available. When I travel, I take with me the foods that I know are healthy for me. When I eat out, I make sure the restaurant menu has healthy options.

I also plan time to work out by getting up early and sometimes saying no to other things. I'm not legalistic, but I do have to be disciplined. I used to hate the idea of exercise programs and was convinced I didn't have time for them. But God showed me that if I didn't get stronger and healthier, it would prevent me from fulfilling His calling on my life. It is amazing what we can find time for if we really want to. We all have the same amount of time each day, and what we do with it is up to us.

*Prayerfully decide what you want to do with your time, then plan ahead so you actually do it.* Determine not to let other things steal your time. Order your life instead of letting it order you.

# BUY YOURSELF SOME TIME

*To everything there is a season, and a time for every matter or
purpose under heaven.*

ECCLESIASTES 3:1

Does time feel too short to you, even when you plan ahead?
If so, you might consider buying some. No, you can't order
more than a twenty-four-hour day on the internet, but you
can pay someone to do the things that have to be done but
don't necessarily need you to do them.

*If you can afford it, think about hiring someone to do house-
keeping, laundry, or yard work. Consider paying a teen to pull
weeds, and save yourself a few hours.* I believe we should be
frugal but not cheap. We sometimes have to spend money
to make more money. We may have to seek help in some
areas, so we can thrive in the areas in which God wants us
to thrive.

People often want to do new and exciting things but get
stuck in old ways of thinking that prevent progress. We may
think about all the things we want to do and even feel we are
supposed to do, but we get frustrated because we do not have
the time. Those things may never get done unless we spend
some money to buy some time.

My son and daughter-in-law have four sons, ages four to
fifteen years old. My daughter-in-law was constantly going
to the grocery store. When she decided to try home grocery delivery, it changed her life. Yes, this costs a little more
money, but the time she has saved is more valuable than the
little bit of extra money she spends.

I once did a lot of tasks I now pay someone else to do. If I didn't, I wouldn't be writing this book because I would not have the time to do it. If you need to simplify, this may be the answer you've been looking for. Buy some time, and start doing more things you really want to do.

# BE ORGANIZED

*She looks well to how things go in her household, and the bread of idleness (gossip, discontent, and self-pity) she will not eat.*

**PROVERBS 31:27**

When my surroundings are organized and uncluttered, I feel organized. And when they are disorganized, I feel disorganized. My life feels complicated if I don't keep my schedule, home, closet, work space, and other areas organized.

Years ago, getting out of the house in the morning was a challenge. If I did manage to leave on time, it was usually in an irritable rush—not a positive way to start the day. To simplify my life and relieve stress, I decided I needed to be more organized and prepare the night before. *I started picking out my clothes for the next day and making a list of what I needed to leave the house with.* By doing these things in the evening when I did have time, my mornings became simpler and more relaxed. Starting the day stressed out is not a good choice. After kicking off the day in frustration or hurry, we can stay that way all day, and regaining our peace can be difficult.

Some people say "I'm just not organized." But I think anyone can be organized if they make a plan and discipline themselves to stick to it. Not leaving everything to the last minute is one of the first rules of being organized, so I suggest you start there and grow. You'll be amazed at how much you can accomplish and how good you'll feel doing it.

# DISCOVER THE POWER OF
# SIMPLE PRAYER

*Let Your ear now be attentive and Your eyes open to listen to the
prayer of Your servant which I pray before You day and night.*

NEHEMIAH 1:6

Many people feel frustrated and confused in their prayer
life, perhaps because we've come to believe prayer needs
to be eloquent, long, and perfect-sounding to be effective.
Years ago, God challenged me to pray simply, telling Him
my wants or needs in the fewest words possible, yet being
sincere. I think we often get so caught up in our words that
we may forget to release our faith in God—the one to whom
we pray.

The entire nature of faith is simple. There's nothing complicated about it. It simply leans on, relies on, and trusts in
God. It believes God's Word, knows God is faithful, and
realizes that all things are possible with Him (Matthew
19:26).

In Mark 5:21–43, a Jewish religious leader wanted Jesus
to heal his dying daughter, but Jesus got interrupted before
He got to the man's house. Then the man heard that his
daughter had died. Jesus responded, "Don't be afraid; just
believe" (v. 36 NIV). Jesus then went to his house, told the girl
to get up, and she did. "Just believe" is a simple answer, but it
was true in Jesus' day and it is true for us today.

We are to go to God as little children (Luke 18:17). Children don't try to be eloquent or impressive when asking their

parents for something. They are simple and straightforward. Simple prayer helps produce a simple life, so *talk to God in simple terms and in faith, believing He hears you and will answer.*

# CREATE SOME MARGIN

*For David said, The Lord, the God of Israel has given peace and rest to His people.*

**1 CHRONICLES 23:25**

If you're like I am, you don't like to waste one minute of time. You make appointments and calls while you're at the mechanic's or in line to pick up your child at school. This multitasking may sound like a good idea, but it creates stress. When I plan everything too close together, I end up frustrated and rushing around. What we need is margin—extra time added to each task or appointment. Almost everything takes longer than we think. A last-minute call, lost car keys, or a forgotten cell phone can slow us down and complicate things if we pack too much into the schedule.

I used to avoid getting anywhere early with nothing to do but wait. With no margin, I usually ended up late or barely on time—but full of stress. The good news is that I saw the light and now consistently plan extra time for the unexpected. I'm still working on this but am determined to press on, because I refuse to live a complicated life any longer.

It is better to do less with peace than to do more with stress. Where do you need to add margin? *Try adding ten or fifteen minutes to each item on your to-do list. You will probably end up using it, but if not, try resting.* Close your eyes, lay your head back, and relax. It will help prepare you for what's next on your schedule.

# DON'T TAKE ON OTHER PEOPLE'S RESPONSIBILITIES

*So then, each of us will give an account of ourselves to God.*

**ROMANS 14:12** NIV

I have always been a responsible person, so irresponsible people tend to irritate me. I used to resent being responsible for what others neglected to do until God showed me I had a false sense of responsibility and that a lot of what I did was unnecessary.

Do you automatically step up and do whatever needs to be done, and then feel sorry for yourself? If people disappoint you by ignoring their responsibility, you may feel that the only way to avoid more pain is to do everything yourself. But experience has taught me that such reasoning only amplifies the problem. You could be feeding irresponsibility in someone else by doing what they need to do themselves.

We love people and want to help them, but sometimes tough love helps them more than emotional love. Tough love isn't being mean; it just allows people to experience the consequences of their actions instead of rescuing them. Doing someone else's job for them feeds a lazy, immature, irresponsible attitude in them. *Try doing only the things you are responsible for, not what someone else is—unless it's an emergency.* Examine whether you really need to do everything you're doing.

DAY
64

# MAKE SURE YOU'RE REALLY HELPING PEOPLE

*But let every person carefully scrutinize and examine and test his own conduct and his own work.*

GALATIANS 6:4

Some people find their self-worth in taking care of others. Yet too many of them act like martyrs, constantly complaining about having to do so much. But you can't stop them. They don't want help or an answer; they want to complain. I know a woman who talks about the unfairness of having to sacrifice her life for others, yet she still latches on to anyone she can find to care for.

*If you feel trapped in this behavior and want to get out of it, I suggest you identify your true responsibility and give up the rest.* Some people will get angry that you're no longer helping them, but at least you'll regain your life and your peace.

For four years, Dave and I spent time, money, and effort trying to help a wounded person from a dysfunctional home, wanting to see him have a chance at a good life. When we did everything for him, things went well, but when it came time for him to take care of himself, he went back to his old ways.

If you've tried to help someone for years, and they are still not "helped," consider whether they really want help. *You* may want to see change in their life, but *they* have to want it too. Make your life simpler. Help all the people you can, but don't become a professional caretaker who feels used up and burned out.

# LET GO

*But you are not living the life of the flesh, you are living the life of the Spirit, if the [Holy] Spirit of God [really] dwells within you [directs and controls you]. But if anyone does not possess the [Holy] Spirit of Christ, he is none of His [he does not belong to Christ, is not truly a child of God].*

ROMANS 8:9

I am a strong type A personality who was raised in a dysfunctional family by another type A personality, who was a master controller. So as an adult, I also wanted to control everything and everybody. I was clearly living in the flesh. I've come a long way, but I still have to remind myself that God is in control; nobody else is. *Deciding to let go and let God be God is the pathway to simplicity, and I urge you to do it.*

Some evenings, I ask Dave to watch a movie with me. He agrees but sometimes wants to take a shower first. An hour may pass and still no Dave. By then, I am frustrated because he is moving too slow for my timetable. Recently I thought, *Why do I care if Dave is on time to watch the movie?* I now tell him what time I'm starting it and let him do whatever he wants. I enjoy the evening, and when he finally comes in, he asks me what's been happening. Now I am practicing not getting irritated about that.

Dave has also told me he's going to take fifteen minutes to check the sports scores. Sometimes I don't see him again after that. I now shake my head when I realize how many evenings I got upset and nothing ever changed. Now I simply let him do what he wants. I don't try to control him; I do what I want, and our evenings at home are simpler.

# BE FLEXIBLE

*And other seed [of the same kind] fell into good (well-adapted) soil
and brought forth grain, growing up and increasing, and yielded
up to thirty times as much, and sixty times as much, and even a
hundred times as much as had been sown.*

**MARK 4:8**

If your attitude is "My way or no way," you're in for a rough
life. This attitude is not the type of soil that will bring forth
a good harvest. When you're not willing to adapt and adjust,
you're much more likely to be angry or have someone angry
at you. Your life certainly won't be simple.

Pride is at the root of unwillingness to adapt and adjust
to the desires of others. God tells us in His Word that if we
humble ourselves under His mighty hand, He will exalt us
in due time (1 Peter 5:6). If we are willing to do whatever is
necessary to accomplish God's will, at the right time, God
Himself will lift us to a place beyond anything we could do
for ourselves.

Getting our own way is highly overrated. We struggle
and argue to get what we want, but the truth is we are happier when we live to make others happy over ourselves.

It is much simpler to adapt and hold your peace than to
fight and end up in strife. Strife or conflict is the result of our
trying to get the things we want instead of asking God for
them and waiting for His perfect timing (James 4:1–2).

I struggled with this for years but finally decided peace
was much more important than pride. *I recommend you be
ready to adapt if you truly desire to simplify your life.*

# ACCEPT WHAT YOU CAN'T CHANGE

*Do you know how God controls the clouds and makes his lightning flash? Do you know how the clouds hang poised, those wonders of him who has perfect knowledge?*

**JOB 37:15-16** NIV

God is perfect in knowledge, and often only He can do what needs to be done in our lives. Trying to do what you can't do only produces frustration and feelings of failure. This is why it's important for us to learn what we can do and what we aren't able to do. We are partners with God, and in a partnership, each party has a part. The partnership works best when each one does what they are good at. When we have a need we cannot meet for ourselves, God is always there to help us. Sometimes, He helps us in sovereign ways, and sometimes He uses other people to help us.

I tried to change many things about myself, other people, and my circumstances that only God could change—my husband, my children, my neighbor, myself, and other situations. I kept failing, but I also kept trying, often to no avail. I said I was trusting God, but I actually trusted myself more. God's ways and timing are not the same as ours, so when we get tired of waiting, we usually take matters into our own hands. This ends up only making our wait longer and frustrates us more.

As the old saying reminds us, "Don't spin your wheels and go nowhere." You can simplify your life by no longer trying to do what you can't do. *You do not have to be a superhero.* Give yourself permission to be who you are—an imperfect human being who needs help, relying on God to send you the help you need.

# CHANGE WHAT YOU CAN CHANGE

*Remember that [by submission] you magnify God's work, of which men have sung.*

JOB 36:24

Submitting to God is a powerfully effective way to simplify a cluttered, complicated life. Often God changes things and we resist, but submission is much better. Some people say they hate change when really they love the results of change; they just don't like the process.

When things change, we often feel disoriented for a time. When we step out boldly to make changes, we risk the possibility of failure. The change may not be as good as what we have, but then again, it could be much better. The only way to find out is to try.

Have you thought about changing something but never taken steps to do it? Good intentions can become a deeper and deeper rut. God looks for bravehearted souls who hear His voice and follow His leading.

The only way to discover what you can have is to give up what you currently have. Increase always demands investment. I had to leave a secure church staff position to start my own ministry. It was a frightening, lonely time for me, but deep down I knew I needed to make a change. I had to invest what I had, and I ended up with much more than I gave up.

*Make regular, necessary changes that will help keep your life simple.* As you prune (cut) things off that need to go, you unclutter your life and make room for the fresh and new.

# SET REALISTIC EXPECTATIONS

*And now, Lord, what do I wait for and expect? My hope and expectation are in You.*

**PSALMS 39:7**

If we expect from another human being something we should only expect from God, we will end up disappointed and frustrated. *Ask God for what you want and need, and trust Him to work through whomever He chooses to answer your prayer.* The Bible says Jesus knew human nature and did not trust Himself to people (John 2:24–25). He fully understood how imperfect people can be in terms of meeting our expectations. He kept good relationships but was also realistic about human shortcomings.

I got hurt several times in the past, wanting people to give me what only God could give—my sense of self-worth and value. I looked to people to make me feel good about myself when, in reality, I needed to find my true value in God and His love for me. When we place our hope and expectation in Him, we will not be disappointed.

People usually don't intend to hurt us, but we all hurt and disappoint one another simply because we have inherent weaknesses. We are naturally selfish and tend to do what is best for ourselves instead of other people. As we mature spiritually, we can overcome these selfish tendencies, but while we are in the process of changing, we will make mistakes.

Make the decision to put your expectations in God. Trust Him for what you want and need, and it will make life a lot simpler.

# TAKE ONE STEP AT A TIME

*But let endurance and steadfastness and patience have full play and do a thorough work, so that you may be [people] perfectly and fully developed [with no defects], lacking in nothing.*

JAMES 1:4

Anything that grows and changes does so progressively. When a seed is planted in the ground, it doesn't immediately sprout and produce fruit. The farmer must be patient and so must we. God helps us defeat our enemies little by little (Deuteronomy 7:22); rarely does He wipe them all out in one fell swoop. As we are diligent to study His Word, He changes us into His image, little by little (2 Corinthians 3:18). We inherit the promises of God through faith and patience (Hebrews 10:36).

Being impatient only tends to make us miserable, and it does not make God hurry. His timing is perfect, and the best thing we can do is make the decision to enjoy our journey through life. Enjoy every step of your progress, or you will waste a lot of your life being frustrated about something you cannot change.

Expecting instant gratification or quick change is almost always unrealistic and will leave you frustrated and disappointed. *If you desire to simplify your life, then understand that everything is a process that takes time.* This will help you relax and enable you to enjoy your life.

The fruit of patience is a seed resting in you, and as you wait with a good attitude, it develops and grows. You may not be where you want to be, but you are making progress. That's something to celebrate and enjoy.

# PROTECT YOURSELF FROM BURNOUT

*Happy (blessed, fortunate, enviable) is the man who finds skillful and godly Wisdom, and the man who gets understanding [drawing it forth from God's Word and life's experiences].*

**PROVERBS 3:13**

Have you ever suffered from burnout? I have, and it's not an experience I want to repeat. I believe the main reason people burn out is that they don't use wisdom as they steward their time and energy. *Wise people acknowledge their limitations and avoid trying to be superhuman.* God has no limitations and can do through us things we can never do on our own, but each of us can and will burn out if we don't use wisdom in our scheduling and the commitments we make.

Jesus said that when we are weary and burdened we should go to Him and He will give us rest (Matthew 11:28). One way He gives rest is by showing us what we need to change in our lives.

Burnout doesn't happen overnight. If you find yourself extra cranky, dragging into work and leaving early, caring less about things that were once important to you, or feeling physically sick though there's no clear diagnosis of what may be wrong with you, you may be experiencing symptoms of burnout. Some people ignore the warning signs and keep pushing until their burnout is so severe they never recover. They give up on things God truly intended them to do simply because they were not realistic about their own needs. The simple way to live is to pace yourself, so you can accomplish a lot in life and not get derailed through burnout.

# SPEND SOME TIME ALONE

*My people shall dwell in a peaceable habitation, in safe dwellings,
and in quiet resting-places.*

ISAIAH 32:18

Being alone and enjoying quiet time is very healing to our
souls. Everyone needs regular time to reflect and allow the
soul to quiet down. Our minds need to rest; they need the
peace found in solitude. Our emotions need time to settle,
level out, and recover from daily life. When we feel weary, as
though we cannot go on, solitude helps us find the determination we need to finish our course with joy.

Jesus regularly went into the mountains to be alone. He
was refreshed and strengthened through solitude. In the
quiet, we give God an opportunity to speak to us, and we are
reassured of the direction He wants us to take in life.

Without solitude, my life can seem out of control. My
emotions can feel frazzled, and I can feel overwhelmed and
confused by everyone's expectations. But after a little quiet
time—some time alone in prayer and meditation—everything
changes. I find wisdom and direction in times of solitude, and
these times alone refresh and restore my soul.

I absolutely love solitude and the peace I find in those times.
They prepare me for the rest of life. *Make the effort to carve out
time in your day, week, or month to find some solitude.* Get up
extra early and watch the sun come up with God. Find a quiet
spot at a park and enjoy the beauty of God's creation. Whatever
you do, I urge you to cultivate solitude because it is truly where
you find the answers to an uncluttered life that can be enjoyed.

# KEEP ETERNITY IN MIND

*Set your minds and keep them set on what is above (the higher things), not on the things that are on the earth.*

**COLOSSIANS 3:2**

Many people are concerned only with today or with their immediate future. We think and plan in temporal terms, but God thinks and plans in eternal terms. We are more interested in what seems good right now and what produces immediate results. God has an eternal purpose for our lives.

Ecclesiastes 3:11 says:

He has made everything beautiful in its time. He also has planted eternity in men's hearts and minds [a divinely implanted sense of a purpose working through the ages which nothing under the sun but God alone can satisfy], yet so that men cannot find out what God has done from the beginning to the end.

One way to simplify our lives is to stop planning so much and to trust God as He guides us day by day. When we follow God, He leads us to do not only what is best for right now but also what is best for eternity. God sees and understands what we don't. He wants us to trust Him and His perfect timing.

When we keep our focus on the bigger eternal picture, we eliminate much of the time we waste worrying about what isn't happening as we believe it should. Wanting to know everything ahead of time is often our way of taking care of ourselves. *Give up reasoning and enjoy the beautiful, simple, powerful life God has waiting for you,* as well as the eternal blessings that come from trusting His will for your life.

## DAY 74 — PRACTICE DAILY DISCIPLINE

*Therefore I always exercise and discipline myself [mortifying my body, deadening my carnal affections, bodily appetites, and worldly desires, endeavoring in all respects] to have a clear (unshaken, blameless) conscience, void of offense toward God and toward men.*

**ACTS 24:16**

Sir William Osler said, "Live neither in the past nor in the future, but let each day's work absorb your entire energies, and satisfy your widest ambition."

Duties we ignore can accumulate and soon feel overwhelming, but daily discipline keeps us in a place to handle life peaceably. Hebrews 12:11 says that no discipline seems joyous in the present moment, but later on it yields the peaceable fruit of righteousness. In other words, doing the right thing may be a challenge and require discipline in the present, but the knowledge that we have done what we were supposed to do ultimately gives us peace.

Daily discipline protects us from suddenly finding we have more to do than is humanly possible. Putting off things that need to be done now does not prevent them from needing to be done. It only adds today's duties to tomorrow. Soon, life becomes so frustrating and overwhelming that we become depressed and discouraged.

Discipline means we must say no to fleshly desires. The apostle Paul said, "I die daily" (1 Corinthians 15:31). He did not mean that he daily experienced physical death, but he did say no to himself regularly if what he desired did not agree with what the Holy Spirit was leading him to do or with his conscience.

*It's never too late to start being disciplined. It may not be comfortable or pleasant at first, but give it a try, and soon you will be enjoying a peaceful, simple life.*

# KNOW THAT GOD IS ON YOUR SIDE

*Then shall my enemies turn back in the day that I cry out; this I
know, for God is for me.*

**PSALM 56:9**

I have read that 10 percent of the people we encounter will
not like us. Most of the time, we can't do anything to change
their minds about us.

The truth is, God is for us, and since He is so mighty
and awesome, it really does not matter much who is against
us (Romans 8:31). We need to focus on who is on our side
instead of thinking about who is against us.

Even if someone doesn't like you, many people do love
and accept you. Life is much more enjoyable when you keep
your mind on them. I encourage you to practice meditating
on what you do have, not what you are missing. As a believer,
you have God. He promises never to leave us or forsake us,
so we are never without Him, and He is more than enough.

When you hear someone does not like you or is unhappy
with you, don't let it upset you. Stay focused on Jesus; He's
your best friend, anyway.

*If you are facing a tremendous challenge right now, one you
feel is too much for you, take a moment and say these words out
loud: "God is for me, and since He is for me, I can do whatever
I need to do in life."*

The Holy Spirit walks alongside you. He is the Standby
and the Helper who we can always rely on. You are never
alone.

# REMEMBER: YOU ARE MORE THAN A CONQUEROR

*Yet amid all these things we are more than conquerors and gain a surpassing victory through Him Who loved us.*

**ROMANS 8:37**

If we begin believing life is too much for us and adopt a "give up" attitude, we make a big mistake and buy into a lie. This complicates our lives. The truth is, we are more than conquerors through Christ who loves us (Romans 8:37). To me, being more than a conqueror means I know when I begin to go through a trial or difficult circumstances that I will have the victory. We don't have to worry or be afraid. God is on our side, and we are more than conquerors. We may feel like David in the Bible, standing before Goliath with nothing more than a slingshot, but we have the assurance that God is with us.

Nothing in creation can separate us from the love of God found in Jesus unless we allow it to do so. When you feel overwhelmed, say, "God loves me, and I am more than a conqueror through Him." Don't believe the devil's lies when he tries to tell you that you won't make it this time. *Stop right now and intentionally recall victories God has given you in the past.* At other times you probably felt you couldn't go on, yet you are still here. That is a testimony in itself. You are an overcomer!

Be positive. Think victory. Believe that God, working in you, is enabling you to do whatever you need to do. This kind of attitude helps you enjoy life at all times.

# PRAY BEFORE YOU HAVE A CRISIS

*Let my prayer come before You and really enter into Your presence; incline Your ear to my cry!*

**PSALM 88:2**

In 1 Timothy 1:12, the apostle Paul thanked God for giving him the strength he needed to handle every situation in life. I believe he did this regularly, not necessarily because of emergencies but as a matter of habit. Praying in advance of a crisis gets us the help we need before we need it, showing that we depend on God and trust Him to take care of things we don't even know about yet.

We release our faith through prayer. *Don't wait until you need faith to try to develop it.* That may be too late. Do it before you're in a situation that requires it. Each morning I pray God will help me throughout the day. I ask God to release His angels assigned to me, to go ahead of me and prepare my way. I usually have plans for each day, but unexpected situations sometimes arise, and I want to be ready for them. When this happens in your life, you can be ready, too, if you pray early and have the help you will need already waiting for you.

Praying before you have an emergency is like putting money in the bank. When you have done it, an unexpected car problem won't upset you. You have provided a way to continue living a simple, joy-filled life *before* you experience a need. Start putting some prayers in reserve today. Fill up your prayer tank, and you will avoid living your life reacting to emergencies. Instead, you will be spiritually prepared for them.

# LIVE WITH A CLEAR CONSCIENCE

*But if your eye is unsound, your whole body will be full of darkness.
If then the very light in you [your conscience] is darkened, how
dense is that darkness!*

MATTHEW 6:23

Nothing complicates life like a guilty conscience. It pressures
us and prevents us from being able to truly live. We may try to
ignore it, but it constantly whispers to us, reminding us that we
have not done right. We should always strive to keep our conscience free of offense toward God and toward other people.

There are only two ways to live with a conscience uncluttered by guilt. The first is to do what is right. If we fail in
that, we move to the second choice, which is to be quick to
repent, admit our sins, and ask for God's forgiveness—and
for other people's, if necessary.

A guilty conscience hinders our faith and worship, putting a stumbling block between us and God until we deal
with our feelings of guilt in a godly way. When we sin against
other people, we will feel guilty when we are with them until
we resolve the situation by apologizing. There is no harder
pillow than a guilty conscience. We will toss and turn at
night if our conscience condemns us and we try to ignore it.

Take some time to examine your heart today. Are there
people you aren't speaking to? Have you wronged anyone?
Are there misunderstandings or hard feelings you need to
put to rest with a friend? *Work to remedy these broken relationships.* Your conscience will be clear, and your free, easy
fellowship with God will be restored.

# KNOW WHAT IT MEANS TO BE RIGHTEOUS

*The heavens declare His righteousness, and all the peoples see His glory.*

PSALM 97:6

Some people have an overactive conscience. They habitually feel guilty, but not necessarily because they have done something wrong. They just feel something *about* them is wrong. To overcome this, study what the Bible has to say about God's righteousness. Then you won't try to earn righteousness through good works.

It is so important to know the difference between your *who* and your *do*. My children may not always do what I want, but they never stop being my children, and I never stop loving them. God is the same way, only better. He gives us right standing with Him when we receive Jesus as our Savior (2 Corinthians 5:21). He imputes it to us, or credits it to our account (Romans 4:11). He views us as righteous, which makes us acceptable to Him, and being made right through our faith in Him is the only way we can fellowship with Him—because light cannot fellowship with darkness (2 Corinthians 6:14).

Since God in His mercy has made us righteous, we can learn right behavior. This process takes time, but gradually our *do* (our behavior) improves. Meanwhile, we need to remember *who* we are in Christ. We are God's children. He knows each one of us, loves us, and understands us.

Simplify your life by studying and understanding what the Bible says about righteousness, or you will always feel bad about yourself. Guilty feelings are complicated and not easy to live with. *Put on the simple garment of righteousness, and start living the life Jesus purchased for you through His death and resurrection.*

# RECEIVE GOD'S GRACE

*But He gives us more and more grace (power of the Holy Spirit, to meet this evil tendency and all others fully). That is why He says, God sets Himself against the proud and haughty, but gives grace [continually] to the lowly (those who are humble enough to receive it).*

JAMES 4:6

Grace is the power of the Holy Spirit, which He offers to us free of charge, enabling us to do with ease what we could never do in our own strength with any amount of effort. Scripture encourages us to receive not only grace but *more* grace. Where sin increases, grace increases much more (Romans 5:20). God has enough grace to meet all our needs. All we need to do is ask for it and learn to live in it.

When we attempt to do things in our flesh (apart from God's grace), we use our energy trying to do what only God can do. This produces frustration, and we end up working in opposition to grace. We can't live with a little self-effort and a little grace, because these two cancel each other out. When I feel frustrated, I remind myself I am not receiving God's grace for the task at hand.

Frustration, complication, and misery are available in abundance, but so is God's grace. We need to humble ourselves under His mighty hand, because this is how we position ourselves to receive His help (James 4:10). We need to admit that we can't do things without God, and ask God to help us.

Grace is the only thing that can change us into what God desires us to be, which is to be like Him. *Unclutter your life by learning how to receive grace in every situation.* Without it, everything becomes hard, difficult, and usually impossible.

# WATCH YOUR MOUTH

*Keep your tongue from evil and your lips from speaking deceit.*
**PSALM 34:13**

One way to greatly simplify your life is to stop going through life saying whatever you want to say whenever you want to say it. James 1:26 says, "Those who consider themselves religious and yet do not keep a tight rein on their tongues deceive themselves, and their religion is worthless" (NIV).

Ponder this scripture, and think about the "religious" people in the world (those who abide by religious rules and regulations apart from a personal relationship with God) who do not discipline their tongues. They frequently speak in negative terms, gossip, criticize, judge, murmur, and complain. They go to church but do not discipline what they say. The Bible makes clear that their religious service is worthless.

Many of our problems are rooted in our words. The power of life and death is in the tongue, and we must be satisfied with the results of our words (Proverbs 18:21). I urge you to be careful about what you say. James 3:2 says that those who never say the wrong thing can control their whole body and, I believe, affect their destiny.

Are you dissatisfied with your life? Perhaps what you have now is the result of what you have said in the past. *Offer your mouth to God to be used in His service,* and you will be on the road to a simpler, better life.

# LET GOD FIGHT YOUR BATTLES

*The Lord will fight for you, and you shall hold your peace and remain at rest.*

**EXODUS 14:14**

Complication often occurs when we don't trust God to fight our battles for us. The Israelites were between the Red Sea and the Egyptian army, which was a frightening place to be. They were crying and wanting to run away, but God sent a message through Moses, saying, "The Lord will fight for you, and you shall hold your peace and remain at rest" (Exodus 14:14).

When three armies came against King Jehoshaphat and the people of Judah, their first inclination was to be afraid. But they intentionally sought God, and He told them, "Do not be afraid or discouraged because of this vast army. For the battle is not yours, but God's" (2 Chronicles 20:15 NIV).

How do you see the battles you face? Are they yours or God's? Remember, it's not what happens in life that makes it so complicated; it's the way we approach it that produces stress and strife. The attitudes and mindsets we embrace determine whether we experience peace or turmoil.

Jehoshaphat worshipped God. As he went into battle, he sent people ahead of the army to sing and praise God (2 Chronicles 20:21). Soon the enemy armies became confused and slaughtered one another (2 Chronicles 20:22).

Do you want to live in confusion, or would you rather confuse the enemy? *Begin to worship, praise, and sing, especially when you have a problem.* God will fight your battles for you, and you can continue enjoying your life while you wait for His victory.

# RUN FROM TEMPTATION

*All of you must keep awake (give strict attention, be cautious and active) and watch and pray, that you may not come into temptation. The spirit indeed is willing, but the flesh is weak.*

**MATTHEW 26:41**

We all wish we were never tempted to do wrong things, but that is not reality. Matthew 18:7 says temptation must come, but why? If we are never tempted to do wrong, we can never exercise our free will to do right. God does not want robots or puppets serving Him; He wants free people who *choose* to serve Him. He sets before us life and death and urges us to choose life (Deuteronomy 30:19).

*The moment you feel tempted to do wrong, say no and get away from the temptation.* If you have a problem with alcohol, don't go to bars. If you have a problem with drugs, don't spend the day with people who get high. If you abuse sweets, don't keep cookies, candy, and cake in your house.

Sometimes we say we don't want to do something, and we pray for God to deliver us, yet we continue making provision for the very things that tempt us. Maybe we really don't want to be as free as we say we do. We must be honest with ourselves and realize that the flesh is weak.

The apostle Paul says to "make no provision for [indulging] the flesh [put a stop to thinking about the evil cravings of your physical nature] to [gratify its] desires (lusts)" (Romans 13:14). Avoid temptation by getting the things that tempt you off your mind and out of sight.

# LISTEN TO WHAT PEOPLE SAY

*He who goes about as a talebearer reveals secrets; therefore associate not with him who talks too freely.*

**PROVERBS 20:19**

People who talk too much often have problems you may be better off not being involved with. Avoiding encounters with them helps simplify our lives.

When people have no discipline over their mouths, they usually lack discipline in other areas too. In our close relationships, it is best to choose those who urge us to come up higher in our choices. Spending excessive time with, and opening your heart to, those who pull you down is not wise. Think about who your friends are and start really listening to them, because you can tell a lot about a person's character by what they say. *Avoid people who gossip.* If they gossip about someone else to you, they will gossip about you to others.

When people talk too freely, they often don't follow through on what they say because they make commitments before counting the costs. They will fill your ears with verbal clutter and often disappoint you over and over, causing frustration. You are the only one who can simplify your life by avoiding these people. I am not suggesting that we be rude, but we can't let people influence our lives negatively just to prevent their feelings being hurt.

The best thing is to choose your friends wisely. I have simplified my life by making a few adjustments in this area myself. Guard your heart with all diligence, for out of it flow the issues of life (Proverbs 4:23).

# PRACTICE GENEROSITY

*There are those who [generously] scatter abroad, and yet increase more; there are those who withhold more than is fitting or what is justly due, but it results only in want. The liberal person shall be enriched, and he who waters shall himself be watered.*

**PROVERBS 11:24-25**

One of the wisest things anyone can do is be generous. When we help other people, we actually help ourselves even more. To experience the joy of giving is what I call real living. Greed steals life, but generosity releases life, along with amazing joy. I spent many unhappy years being selfish and concerned about what I could get out of life. I cried out to God, asking Him what was wrong, and He showed me that I was selfish and needed to be more generous and more thoughtful toward others.

Look for opportunities to be a blessing, and be aggressively generous. ***Don't just give when you have to, but do more than required.*** Go the extra mile, as Matthew 5:41 teaches.

I heard of a terribly depressed woman who went to her pastor for counseling. He told her to go home, bake three batches of cookies, give them away, and come back the following week for another appointment. The woman never returned. One Sunday after church, he saw her and asked why she didn't return for her appointment. She said she got so happy when she started baking and giving away cookies that she got over her depression!

Many things can cause depression, but I believe one of them is being self-centered and stingy. Do all you can, for as many people as you can, and you will be much happier. Being generous is much simpler than being selfish.

# USE WISDOM

*Hear instruction and be wise, and do not refuse or neglect it.*

**PROVERBS 8:33**

Proverbs 10:23 says wisdom is "pleasure and relaxation" to a person of understanding. Wisdom is choosing to do now what you will be happy with later. Wisdom doesn't spend all its money now but saves some for the future. It doesn't put off today's work until tomorrow. Wisdom is not a procrastinator but instead takes action.

If you want to simplify your life, think about the future and realize that the choices you make today will affect tomorrow. Some people are not able to relax and enjoy life because they are dealing with the messes resulting from not walking in wisdom. I frequently hear people say "I know I shouldn't do this, but…" How can anyone expect a right result from a wrong decision? They are gambling on things turning out right anyway. But wisdom doesn't gamble; it invests. Doing what's right now may not bring pleasure immediately, but it will later on. Some people pay a high price for a cheap thrill, but you can decide not to be one of them.

We make many decisions in our lifetime, and the wiser we are, the better our lives will be. *Simplify your life by asking yourself before you make decisions how they will impact your life later.* Ask yourself if you believe you will be happy with the results later in life. If not, rethink that decision and consider doing something different.

# AVOID DISTRACTION

*Then the cares and anxieties of the world and distractions of the age, and the pleasure and delight and false glamour and deceitfulness of riches, and the craving and passionate desire for other things creep in and choke and suffocate the Word, and it becomes fruitless.*

**MARK 4:19**

Distractions are a form of mental clutter. It's easy for us to get distracted in life; it is not something we have to try to do. We do, however, need to discipline ourselves *not* to get distracted. It seems every person in our life expects something from us. It's confusing to know when to say yes and when to say no. Our spouses, friends, parents, children, other relatives, employers, government, churches, and neighborhood all expect us to do different things. This can be overwhelming and tiring.

While trying to meet all these expectations, we can be distracted from our main goal, which is following God's will and pursuing His purpose for our lives. If you are a people-pleaser, then you know it is not difficult for the devil to distract you. He can easily lead you to dissatisfied people and cause you to spend your life trying to make them happy. I finally realized a lot of the people I was trying to keep happy had already decided they were not going to be happy no matter what anyone did. They were basically miserable, dissatisfied, unhappy—and the devil was using them to make me unhappy.

The Bible teaches us not to get entangled or distracted but to focus on Jesus (Hebrews 12:2). *The more you focus on the truly important things, the simpler your life will be.*

# DON'T GET TRAPPED IN OFFENSE

*Understand [this], my beloved brethren. Let every man be quick to hear [a ready listener], slow to speak, slow to take offense and to get angry.*

JAMES 1:19

A wise person ignores an insult. I once heard a story about Kathryn Kuhlman, a woman who had a wonderful miracle ministry in the mid-1900s. Anyone in the public eye will inevitably deal with people who judge, criticize, and even say and publish things about them that are not true. This happened to Kuhlman frequently, but she refused to get offended because she knew it would be harmful to her relationship with God. Taking offense would steal her joy and not do her any good. People asked her how she could be friendly with people who said such ugly things about her, and she said, "Oh, we are just going to pretend that never happened." She overlooked the offenses.

God promises to be our vindicator if we will do things His way, and His way is to forgive. Has someone hurt your feelings recently? Are you offended? Do you need to forgive someone?

If so, I recommend you do what the Bible says. *Pray for your enemies, bless, and do not curse them* (Luke 6:28). *Decide to forgive and trust God to heal your wounded emotions.* If you see the person who hurt you, do your best to be friendly and treat them the way you believe God wants you to treat them. The quicker you forgive, the less likely you are to develop bitterness in your heart, and the simpler your life will be.

# LIGHTEN UP ON YOURSELF

*Take My yoke upon you and learn of Me, for I am gentle (meek) and
humble (lowly) in heart, and you will find rest (relief and ease and
refreshment and recreation and blessed quiet) for your souls.*

**MATTHEW 11:29**

If you are quick to judge and criticize yourself, consider
reading Matthew 11:28–30. Jesus says He is not harsh, hard,
sharp, or pressing; He is humble, gentle, meek, and lowly.
Since God is not hard on us, we don't need to be so hard on
ourselves. Do you need a second chance? God gave Jonah
and Peter one, so expect Him to give you one too.

*Ask God for a second chance—or for more than that.* He is
full of mercy, and He is long-suffering. His loving-kindness
never fails or comes to an end. If we keep an account of our
shortcomings and failures, we will feel oppressed. Jesus
came to lift burdens, but we must be willing to believe He
is greater than our mistakes. I don't believe God is as hard
to please as we often think. He knew all about us before
He invited us into relationship with Him. If your life seems
complicated, perhaps you need to give yourself a break.
Receive God's mercy for yourself, and you will also be able
to extend it to others.

God sees your heart and will work with anyone who
refuses to give up. Keep pressing on, and let go of the past—
whether it's ten years ago or five minutes ago. The point is, if
a situation has passed, then let it go and press on.

# MAKE A FRESH START

*It is because of the Lord's mercy and loving-kindness that we are not consumed, because His [tender] compassions fail not. They are new every morning; great and abundant is Your stability and faithfulness.*
**LAMENTATIONS 3:22–23**

Hopelessness is a burden none of us needs to endure, because with God we can always have a fresh start. He is the God of new beginnings. It's never too late to pray and ask for God's help, guidance, or forgiveness. The devil wants us to feel hopeless. He plants words such as *always* and *never* in our minds. He tells you that you *always* mess up and can *never* overcome your bad choices. Remember to look to God's Word for truth, because the devil is a liar.

The Bible is filled with stories about people who experienced new beginnings. Receiving Jesus as our Savior is the ultimate new beginning. When He comes to live in our hearts, we become new creatures who learn a new way of living. Ephesians 4:23 says that we are to constantly renew our minds and attitudes. Whenever you begin to think it's too late for you to have a good life, good relationships, or hope for the future, renew your mind according to God's Word right away. *Choose to think according to His Word, not according to how you feel.* Nobody is a failure unless they choose to stop trying. Life gets a lot sweeter and easier if we say "I will do my best today, and I trust God will do the rest. Tomorrow I'll begin again, and I will never quit or give up."

# TRUST GOD

*In peace I will both lie down and sleep, for You, Lord, alone make
me dwell in safety and confident trust.*

PSALM 4:8

If you want an uncluttered life, one way to do it is to develop
more trust in God and learn to rely on Him in childlike
faith.

Children usually don't suffer from distrust. They climb
tall trees, run down steep hills, and jump off high diving
boards. They trust their parents to catch them, or at least to
pick them up if they fall. That's the same kind of trust God
wants from us.

If we trust God, we know that even if things don't go
as we hope, God will have a better plan. He has the future
mapped out, and He knows the answer to everything. His
Word promises He will take care of us if we trust in Him
(Psalm 37:5).

When we don't trust God, we allow fear and worry to come
in, and we carry burdens we weren't meant to bear alone. By
trusting Him, we remove those doubts. We can trust God's
faithfulness and be confident He will not let us down.

Trusting God brings a supernatural rest into our souls,
allowing us to live simply and freely—the way He wants us
to. Trust doesn't just appear in our lives; it grows as we take
steps of faith and experience God's faithfulness. Oswald
Chambers wrote, "Faith is unutterable trust in God, trust
which never dreams that He will not stand by us." *Ask God
to help you develop a deep trust in Him.*

# BE THE PERSON WHO LIVES INSIDE YOU

*Since by your obedience to the Truth through the [Holy] Spirit you have purified your hearts for the sincere affection of the brethren, [see that you] love one another fervently from a pure heart.*

**1 PETER 1:22**

We all have someone living inside us called the "hidden person of the heart." This refers to who we are in the core of our being, and if we are going to enjoy life, we must like that person. I cannot overestimate the importance of having a right heart. God looks on the heart (1 Samuel 16:7). He is not pleased with an evil heart but loves a righteous one. God delights in people who want to do what's right even if they don't always succeed. I believe God would rather have someone with a right heart who makes mistakes than someone with perfect performance and a wicked heart.

God also delights in a peaceful heart, one that's not anxious or upset. This sense of peace proves they are trusting Him in all things. When our hearts lean one way, but we pretend to feel another way or act in a way that's not true to who we really are, it makes life extremely complicated. Have you ever heard the phrase *pure and simple*? I used to keep those words on a sign on my desk to remind myself that if I wanted a simple life, I had to keep a pure heart.

Get to know the person you really are deep inside. Do some soul-searching, and ask yourself if what you show people is the real you or someone you have invented. *If you are pretending to be someone you're not, ask God to purify your heart.*

111

# STAY ENCOURAGED

*Therefore we do not become discouraged (utterly spiritless, exhausted, and wearied out through fear). Though our outer man is [progressively] decaying and wasting away, yet our inner self is being [progressively] renewed day after day.*

2 CORINTHIANS 4:16

Babies learn to walk by taking one step at a time. As they're learning, they frequently fall down. If they became so discouraged that they quit trying, they would never learn to walk. We may get discouraged, but let's remember that everyone has setbacks—which are often designed to check our character and faith. Will we give up, or will we get up and try again? The Bible says the righteous man falls seven times and rises again (Proverbs 24:16). None of us manifests perfection while in fleshly bodies.

When God gives us instructions, He often shows us only one step at a time. It's natural for us to want the entire blueprint, but that's not how God works. If we take that one step, we are given another, until we finally reach our destination. Many people refuse to take one step until they have their entire future figured out. They usually end up frustrated and discouraged. *I urge you not to live this way. Do what God leads you to do, one step at a time.*

Even those willing to take one step at a time will make mistakes and have to try again. If we say we trust God, we must trust Him all along the way. It is not about the destination as much as the journey.

Discouragement clutters our lives because it comes with other negative emotions. Faith is simple. We do what we can do, and trust God to do what we cannot. This attitude leaves us free to enjoy life.

# LET HOPE HOLD ON TO YOU

*Return to the stronghold [of security and prosperity], you prisoners of hope; even today do I declare that I will restore double your former prosperity to you.*

**ZECHARIAH 9:12**

Have you ever heard of "prisoners of hope"? Do you know what this phrase means? I believe prisoners of hope are those who refuse to stop hoping no matter how desperate their circumstances are. Prisoners of hope are swept up and locked in to hope; they just can't get away from it. They are compelled to hope in God and believe something good is going to happen.

I think Abraham must have been a prisoner of hope. Romans 4:18 tells us he had no human reason to hope, yet he hoped, in faith, that God's promise would manifest in his life. Hope deferred makes the heart sick (Proverbs 13:12), and it causes depression, discouragement, and despair. When you have hope, you intentionally become positive in your thoughts and attitudes. Hope also speaks positively. Hope believes all things are possible with God (Matthew 19:26), and it expects good news at any moment. Hope says, "Something good is going to happen to me today."

A positive attitude makes life simpler. It relieves stress and puts a smile on your face. It is the attitude God wants us to have, so He can work His will in our life. If we are going to walk with God, we must agree with Him. After all, He knows the thoughts and plans He has for us, thoughts of welfare and peace, to give us hope in our final outcome (Jeremiah 29:11). *Become a prisoner of hope today.*

# RESIST THE ENEMY

*So be subject to God. Resist the devil [stand firm against him], and he will flee from you.*

JAMES 4:7

James 4:7 teaches that if we submit ourselves to God and resist the devil, he will flee. If we don't resist the devil's lies and temptations, he will eventually rule over us in every area. He is an aggressive enemy, and we need to be aggressive in resisting him.

The devil wants our lives to be miserable and complicated. He endeavors to steal our joy, peace, and every good thing Jesus died to give us. Decide today that you will exercise your rights as a child of God and enjoy the life He has given you. We often think God's will for us will automatically happen, but this is not true. We need to exercise our faith, which includes resisting the devil.

If someone were breaking into your home at night, would you just lie in bed and assume God would take care of it? Of course not! You'd jump up, grab something to use for protection, pray, and call for help. You would aggressively protect yourself and your family from the intruder. Why don't we behave the same way when the devil tries to break into our lives and steal God's good plan?

It's time to be more aggressive against the enemy. Remember that God in you is greater than any foe. *The simple thing to do is to resist the devil at his onset (when he first comes against you). The longer you wait, the more of a foothold he will gain.*

# STAY STRONG IN GOD

*The strong spirit of a man sustains him in bodily pain or trouble.*

**PROVERBS 18:14**

We want to be strong in God at all times, and we build up our spiritual reserves over time by regularly spending time with Him, praying and studying His Word. It's foolish to wait until you need to pick up something heavy and then quickly try to build some muscle. You would never start working out at the gym one day and expect to lift three times your weight the next. Similarly, we gradually build spiritual strength to endure the trials of life without weakening.

I have discovered that if I stay spiritually strong, many situations no longer bother me. Some of these things once upset me because I wasn't strong enough in God to resist them properly or to even look at them from the right perspective. Our mindset toward life's challenges has a lot to do with how they affect us emotionally and how we handle them.

Always being under condemnation, feeling burdened, or experiencing loss of peace or joy can happen for complicated reasons, and those reasons require our attention. Staying spiritually strong may seem like hard work, but it is actually much simpler than always feeling overwhelmed by what is going on in life. *Be strong in the Lord and in the power of His might* (Ephesians 6:10).

# NEVER GIVE UP

*Many a man proclaims his own loving-kindness and goodness, but a faithful man who can find?*

**PROVERBS 20:6**

Not many people know how to be faithful and see things through to completion. They think giving up makes life easier, but not living up to commitments only complicates each day. Unfaithful people end up with a lot of unfinished projects and a lifetime of changes in their jobs, churches, and relationships. Their lives become more difficult than they would have been had these people remained faithful and finished what they started.

Many people give up on their marriages when the going is rough. They get a divorce, they marry someone else, and the cycle starts again. Even if the grass is greener on the other side, it still needs to be mowed. Any relationship worth having will have imperfections and need work. If we cannot work through conflict, we will never have good relationships.

If Dave had given up on me and our marriage, I might not be teaching God's Word all over the world today. Many people are diamonds in the rough with tremendous capability. They just need someone to stick with them while they are shaped and polished. God is faithful, and we need to be faithful too. *I encourage you to pray long and hard before giving up on anything.* There may be times when quitting is the only option, but often, it is the devil's trick to keep us frustrated and miserable. Stay faithful to what you've promised to do and believe that God will reward you for it.

# DECIDE TO ENJOY LIFE

*You will show me the path of life; in Your presence is fullness of joy, at Your right hand there are pleasures forevermore.*

**PSALM 16:11**

What is your outlook on life? With what mindset do you approach it? As I mentioned earlier, our problem isn't life itself; it's our approach to life that causes difficulty. Two people can have the same problem. One will be happy while the other is depressed. Again, the problem itself isn't the issue; it's the way we *view* the problem.

Our approach to life is our own decision. Nobody can make us unhappy if we decide to be happy. If someone we know makes a bad choice and is miserable, we don't have to be unhappy too. Perhaps I have done my best in a situation, but a friend is still angry and dissatisfied. Does their bad attitude mean I have to lose my joy? Of course not! But I will have to decide not to let them steal it. They get to choose how they will approach life, and I can choose how I will approach it. They may decide to believe the worst, but I can decide to believe the best. It's easy to see which of us will be happy and enjoy life.

Are you positive, believing the best, ready to show mercy and forgiveness to those who hurt you? Or are you depressed, discouraged, and discontent because everything didn't go your way? *Pick your battles wisely, and you will enjoy a life of simplicity.* Having a positive outlook is much easier than having a negative one.

117

# BE HUMBLE

*Therefore, as God's chosen people, holy and dearly loved, clothe yourselves with compassion, kindness, humility, gentleness and patience.*

**COLOSSIANS 3:12** NIV

Animosity is a wedge between individuals that opens a door for the devil to bring destruction. It is a negative emotion that complicates our lives and hurts our hearts and the hearts of others.

*One way to avoid animosity is to stay away from petty controversies, especially when people don't know what they are talking about.* When a person feels the need to always tell everyone what they think they know, they prove they really don't know much at all. If they did, they would know they need to listen more than they talk. Proverbs 13:10 says contention comes by pride. This means people cannot fight and argue unless pride is present.

Humility is the doorway to a simple yet powerful life lived joyfully. Humble yourself under God's mighty hand, so He may exalt you in due time (1 Peter 5:6). Put on the same attitude and humble mind that Christ demonstrated (Philippians 2:5). Humility values peace more than trying to prove one is right. Humility is the highest virtue and a trait we must fervently seek. It is also an open door to promotion and exaltation from God. A servant of God who avoids strife by being humble will enjoy a life of peace and power.

# MAKE FRIENDS WITH DISCIPLINE

*For God did not give us a spirit of timidity (of cowardice, of craven and cringing and fawning fear), but [He has given us a spirit] of power and of love and of calm and well-balanced mind and discipline and self-control.*

**2 TIMOTHY 1:7**

The word *discipline* usually causes people to groan, but we should actually see it as a good friend that helps us get what we want in life. Discipline helps us do what we know we should do but probably will not do without help. Discipline helps us. You may be thinking, *Yes, but it hurts!* This is true, but it also brings order, good results, and eventually freedom.

One thing that hurts worse than learning discipline is a life that is a never-ending, complicated mess. The pain of changing is always better than the agony of not changing. Ask yourself if you would rather feel bad and be weak all your life or discipline yourself to exercise and enjoy feeling healthy and strong? Would you like to continue eating junk food and have bad health, or discipline yourself to change to healthier foods and enjoy good health and long life? Would you like to continue living paycheck to paycheck, or get out of debt and be able to pay cash for what you need? Would you like to continue living in a mess, or do you want your home to be neat, clean, and in order? Then *take the path of discipline to the good things you want in life, because they aren't likely to happen any other way.*

119

# CONCLUSION

I hope and pray this book has helped you begin to simplify your life in many ways. I have personally experienced the joy and peace that come with getting rid of the things that complicate situations, relationships, and the environment around me, and I want this kind of joy and peace for you too.

Simplifying your life is not something that happens immediately, but you can make the decision to simplify today, and you can begin the journey toward an uncluttered life. I believe that every step you take toward simplicity will be a positive one. Even if you can only simplify something that seems small or insignificant right now, that's a step in the right direction. Keep taking steps, and you'll soon begin to reap the benefits of a simpler, less cluttered, less complicated life.

# SOURCE NOTES

The quote from William Osler in chapter 74 is taken from http://www.osler.org.uk/osleriana-2/oslers-aphorisms.

The quote from Oswald Chambers in chapter 91 is taken from https://utmost.org/classic/sublime-intimacy-classic.

### *Do you have a real relationship with Jesus?*

God loves you! He created you to be a special, unique, one-of-a-kind individual, and He has a specific purpose and plan for your life. And through a personal relationship with your Creator—God—you can discover a way of life that will truly satisfy your soul.

No matter who you are, what you've done, or where you are in your life right now, God's love and grace are greater than your sin—your mistakes. Jesus willingly gave His life so you can receive forgiveness from God and have new life in Him. He's just waiting for you to invite Him to be your Savior and Lord.

If you are ready to commit your life to Jesus and follow Him, all you have to do is ask Him to forgive your sins and give you a fresh start in the life you are meant to live. Begin by praying this prayer...

> *Lord Jesus, thank You for giving Your life for me and forgiving me of my sins so I can have a personal relationship with You. I am sincerely sorry for the mistakes I've made, and I know I need You to help me live right.*
>
> *Your Word says in Romans 10:9, "If you declare with your mouth, 'Jesus is Lord,' and believe in your heart that God raised him from the dead, you will be saved" (NIV). I believe You are the Son of God and confess You as my Savior and Lord. Take me just as I am, and work in my heart, making me the person You want me to be. I want to live for You, Jesus, and I am so grateful that You are giving me a fresh start in my new life with You today.*
>
> *I love You, Jesus!*

It's so amazing to know that God loves us so much! He wants to have a deep, intimate relationship with us that grows every day as we spend time with Him in prayer and Bible study. And we want to encourage you in your new life in Christ.

Please visit joycemeyer.org/KnowJesus to request Joyce's book *A New Way of Living*, which is our gift to you. We also have other free resources online to help you make progress in pursuing everything God has for you.

Congratulations on your fresh start in your life in Christ! We hope to hear from you soon.

# ABOUT THE AUTHOR

Joyce Meyer is one of the world's leading practical Bible teachers and a *New York Times*–bestselling author. Joyce's books have helped millions of people find hope and restoration through Jesus Christ. Joyce's program, *Enjoying Everyday Life*, is broadcast on television, radio, and online to millions worldwide in over one hundred languages.

Through Joyce Meyer Ministries, Joyce teaches internationally on a number of topics with a particular focus on how the Word of God applies to our everyday lives. Her candid communication style allows her to share openly and practically about her experiences so others can apply what she has learned to their lives.

Joyce has authored more than 140 books, which have been translated into more than 160 languages, and over 39 million of her books have been distributed worldwide. Bestsellers include *Power Thoughts*; *The Confident Woman*; *Look Great, Feel Great*; *Starting Your Day Right*; *Ending Your Day Right*; *Approval Addiction*; *How to Hear from God*; *Beauty for Ashes*; and *Battlefield of the Mind*.

Joyce's passion to help people who are hurting is foundational to the vision of Hand of Hope, the missions arm of Joyce Meyer Ministries. Each year Hand of Hope provides millions of meals for the hungry and malnourished, installs freshwater wells in poor and remote areas, provides critical relief after natural disasters, and offers free medical and dental care to thousands through their hospitals and clinics worldwide. Through Project GRL, women and children are rescued from human trafficking and provided safe places to receive an education, nutritious meals, and the love of God.

# JOYCE MEYER MINISTRIES
## U.S. & FOREIGN OFFICE ADDRESSES

Joyce Meyer Ministries
P.O. Box 655
Fenton, MO 63026
USA
(636) 349-0303

Joyce Meyer
Ministries—Canada
P.O. Box 7700
Vancouver, BC V6B 4E2
Canada
(800) 868-1002

Joyce Meyer
Ministries—Australia
Locked Bag 77
Mansfield Delivery Centre
Queensland 4122
Australia
(07) 3349 1200

Joyce Meyer
Ministries—England
P.O. Box 1549
Windsor SL4 1GT
United Kingdom
01753 831102

Joyce Meyer
Ministries—South Africa
P.O. Box 5
Cape Town 8000
South Africa
(27) 21-701-1056

Joyce Meyer
Ministries—Francophonie
29 avenue Maurice Chevalier
77330 Ozoir la Ferriere
France

Joyce Meyer
Ministries—Germany
Postfach 761001
22060 Hamburg
Germany
+49 (0)40 / 88 88 4 11 11

Joyce Meyer
Ministries—Netherlands
Lorenzlaan 14
7002 HB Doetinchem
+31 657 555 9789

Joyce Meyer
Ministries—Russia
P.O. Box 789
Moscow 101000
Russia
+7 (495) 727-14-68

# Other Books by Joyce Meyer

Love Out Loud
The Love Revolution
Loving People Who Are Hard
to Love
Making Good Habits, Breaking
Bad Habits
Managing Your Emotions
Making Marriage Work
(previously published as *Help
Me—I'm Married!*)
Me and My Big Mouth!*
The Mind Connection*
Never Give Up!
Never Lose Heart
New Day, New You
Overcoming Every Problem
Overload
The Pathway to Success
The Penny
Perfect Love (previously
published as *God Is Not
Mad at You*)*
Philippians: A Biblical Study
The Power of Being Positive
The Power of Being Thankful
The Power of Determination
The Power of Forgiveness
The Power of Simple Prayer
Power Thoughts
Power Thoughts Devotional
Powerful Thinking
Quiet Times with God Devotional
Reduce Me to Love
The Secret Power of Speaking
God's Word

The Secrets of Spiritual Power
The Secret to True Happiness
Seven Things That Steal Your Joy
Start Your New Life Today
Starting Your Day Right
Straight Talk
Teenagers Are People Too!
Trusting God Day by Day
The Word, the Name, the Blood
Woman to Woman
You Can Begin Again
Your Battles Belong to the Lord*

**Joyce Meyer Spanish Titles**
Auténtica y única (Authentically,
Uniquely You)
Belleza en lugar de cenizas
(Beauty for Ashes)
Buena salud, buena vida (Good
Health, Good Life)
Cambia tus palabras, cambia
tu vida (Change Your Words,
Change Your Life)
El campo de batalla de la mente
(Battlefield of the Mind)
Cómo envejecer sin avejentarse
(How to Age without Getting Old)
Como formar buenos habitos y
romper malos habitos (Making
Good Habits, Breaking Bad
Habits)
La conexión de la mente (The
Mind Connection)
Dios no está enojado contigo
(God Is Not Mad at You)

La dosis de aprobación (The Approval Fix)

Efesios: Comentario biblico (Ephesians: Biblical Commentary)

Empezando tu día bien (Starting Your Day Right)

Hágalo con miedo (Do It Afraid)

Hazte un favor a ti mismo... perdona (Do Yourself a Favor... Forgive)

Madre segura de sí misma (The Confident Mom)

Momentos de quietud con Dios (Quiet Times with God Devotional)

Mujer segura de sí misma (The Confident Woman)

No se afane por nada (Be Anxious for Nothing)

Pensamientos de poder (Power Thoughts)

Sanidad para el alma de una mujer (Healing the Soul of a Woman)

Sanidad para el alma de una mujer, devocionario (Healing the Soul of a Woman Devotional)

Santiago: Comentario bíblico (James: Biblical Commentary)

Sobrecarga (Overload)*

Sus batallas son del Señor (Your Battles Belong to the Lord)

Termina bien tu día (Ending Your Day Right)

Tienes que atreverte (I Dare You)

Usted puede comenzar de nuevo (You Can Begin Again)

Viva amando su vida (Living a Life You Love)

Viva valientemente (Living Courageously)

Vive por encima de tus sentimientos (Living beyond Your Feelings)

* Study Guide available for this title

**Books by Dave Meyer**
Life Lines